# Focus on

# **The Poetry of John Clare:**
## The Everyman Selection

Angela Topping

GREENWICH EXCHANGE
LONDON

**Greenwich Exchange, London**

Focus on
The Poetry of John Clare: The Everyman Selection


First published in Great Britain in 2015


Printed and bound by **imprint**digital.net
Typesetting and layout by Jude Keen Limited, London
Tel: 020 8355 4541
Cover design by December Publications, Belfast
Tel: 028 90286559

Greenwich Exchange Website: www.greenex.co.uk

Cataloguing in Publication Data is available from the British Library.

ISBN-13: 978-1-906075-48-4

*For my husband, Dave*

**Acknowledgements**

Acknowledgements are due to Dr Ira Lightman and Mary Jay for commenting on draft versions of some chapters, Rita Lamb for advice on historical matters, the staff at Clare Cottage for their help and kindness, and the late Matt Simpson who suggested I write the book and discussed it with me before his death in 2009. The settings of John Clare's songs by Gordon Tyrrall, in his album *A Distance from the Town* (Fellside, 2005), inspired me during the writing of this book, as did Pete Morton's song about John Clare on his album *Napoleon Jukebox.*

I am also grateful to Roger Rowe for the most helpful blog he manages on John Clare, and for his continued enthusiasm for Clare's work as shown in the Clare Facebook page we started together.

Thanks are also due to Gladstone's Library, Hawarden, where this book was completed during my Writer-in Residence post in 2013.

There must be something of the peasant in every poet.

*Wallace Stevens*

Clare's affinities and sympathies … are those of a deeply sensitive, solitary man, looking for love in everything he sees and fully aware of love's fragility and human vulnerability.

*Matt Simpson*

# Contents

# Preface

John Clare is a poet of contradictions. He was promoted as a 'peasant poet', which is misleading and patronising: he was a great reader, though mostly self-educated. He spent the last twenty years of his life in an asylum for the insane, but during that time wrote most eloquent poems. He was something of a womaniser when he was a young man, yet he remained true all his life to the memory of his first love, Mary Joyce, from whom he was separated by her father's disapproval. Frail, undersized and bookish, he was not successful at labouring on the land or gardening, and longed to make a living from his poetry. He served in the Northamptonshire Local Militia for four years, joining up because the choice was to receive £2 for volunteering or be called up at random with no payment.

Clare lived from 1793 to 1864, when the Romantic movement was at its height. This movement was a reaction to the rationalism of the eighteenth century; it preferred the world of the imagination. It was a time of great social change, reflected in the revolutions which took place across Europe. This commentary aims to set Clare into context by demonstrating some similarities and differences with other Romantic poets. Clare, for example, admired eighteenth-century poets and sometimes his work echoes Pope. However, his subject matter is often in keeping with the Romantic poets, and, in his best poems, he writes in a personal rather than a public voice.

During Clare's lifetime the Napoleonic Wars were undermining the structure and safety of Europe in a way that foreshadowed the rise of Hitler. The wars followed the French Revolution, which liberal thinkers and first-wave Romantic poets such as William Blake at first supported because they wanted freedom of speech, but turned away from once the Revolution became violent and the Reign of Terror began. Clare is in the second wave of Romantic poets when the power-hungry Corsican, Bonaparte, was a figure inspiring fear, as he set about conquering Europe to create a French Empire.

Nearer home, the working classes were affected powerfully by the Industrial Revolution, and Clare was a first-hand witness to the land enclosures which started in his home village when he was 16 years old. For Clare, the timing is crucial: just as he is becoming an adult and facing adult responsibilities, the land he used to roam as a boy became inaccessible, as did the girl he loved. These circumstances led to Clare associating the enclosures with the fall from Eden. Land first started to be enclosed in Tudor times and in the 1760s Oliver Goldsmith wrote *The Deserted Village*, an elegiac poem about a village which was destroyed to allow a rich man to develop a large garden. Such land enclosures made life in the country more difficult to sustain, at precisely the time that labour was needed in the new cities to serve the machines of the growing industries. Poverty was crippling those who chose to stay in the country, and insanitary conditions in the towns made life difficult there too.

John Clare is not as well known as he deserves to be. In his own time, he was made famous by his first book, but public taste turned away from the fashion for 'rustic' verse and his later works failed to make him the living he had hoped for. Many of his best poems remained unpublished in his lifetime as they were considered too outspoken, too critical of his 'betters' and unsuited for reading by the genteel public. His published work suffered from censorship and even the very titles of his books were changed. His grammar and punctuation, often idiosyncratic, was 'improved' by his publishers, and sometimes the dialect words which give his work part of its distinctiveness, were altered for public consumption. The texts used in the Everyman edition tend to be the 'tidied-up' versions. R.K.R. Thornton made this editorial decision with much thought, though the reader is urged to read Clare's work in the original versions if at all possible. Clare's work is now beginning to be read in the way it deserves and is the focus of some excellent critical commentary.

This monograph is intended as a companion to the Everyman selection of Clare's poems and aims to introduce Clare to new readers as well as to add my voice to the many other commentaries on his work. It generally follows the structure and themes of that selection in which poems are not grouped chronologically but thematically. Occasionally in my commentary, poems have been brought together from different sections, where they suited the chapter thesis more aptly. The Everyman selection is only one of a range of different choices from Clare's vast output. As Paul Farley says in the introduction to his own selection of Clare's poems:

> Organising his work in anything other than a chronological sequence might yield the bird poems of John Clare, the love poems of John Clare, or a book based entirely around his attentiveness to seasons … or the weather … [1]

Different selections of Clare's poetry are available, such as *The Wood is Sweet,* which focuses its attention on Clare's nature poems. The best approach to making a selection would be to work with one particular aspect of his enormous output. Where the Everyman selection falls down is in its attempt to be representative. Thornton states in his introduction:

> I have envisaged my reader as someone new to Clare and sampling what Clare has to offer before (I hope) being fascinated and looking further in his work … The selection is too short to allow for a significant representation of chronological development … there are many I have had to omit which seem as good as the ones I include.

This statement shows that Thornton himself is aware of its limitations. He has also edited *The Midsummer Cushion* with Anne Tibble, for Carcanet (1979), a doorstep of a book which is the collection Clare originally wanted to publish. Instead, the less ambitious book *The Rural Muse* was issued as a result of well-meaning interference by editors and supporters.

The strongest section of the Everyman book is 'Loss and the Politics of Nature', with its excellent choices of some of Clare's most lamenting poems about the damage the enclosures caused. The weakest section is 'Love'. Clare is consistently a love poet, particularly of love going hand in hand with loss. Poems about Mary Joyce are under-represented, and since Clare saw her as his muse, this is a pity. Poems like 'First Love', the 'Ballad' which begins "Where is the Heart" surely deserve a place, as do the delightful song 'Sally Green' and the equally charming and beautifully structured 'Song' which begins "Sweet the pleasures I do find". In the lengthy first section 'A Country Village Year', I would beg a place for 'My Early Home', a beautiful lyric poem, apparently simply describing Helpston, but redolent with the sense of loss in the refrain "my early home was this", which, like Keats' To Autumn', gains in resonance once the context is known. I also lament the fact that only one poem is included on the gypsies, who had a strong influence on the young Clare.

Each chapter in this monograph is free-standing. However, if the book is read through from start to finish, a narrative of Clare's life and concerns emerges. The reader is urged to use this commentary as a starting point. Within the remit of this book it was not possible to write about all of Clare's life or work. As R.K.R. Thornton points out in the introduction to the Everyman selection, Clare is like Hardy in the fact that he wrote a vast number of poems, all of which have value, and different ones stand out for different readers. Likewise, there are a number of excellent biographies, the most scholarly being Jonathan Bate's.[2] The John Clare Society is an excellent source of further information and publications, and Clare Cottage in Helpston, Clare's birthplace is well worth visiting. There is a growing fascination with John Clare's work; at last he seems to be reaching the readership he deserved, denied to him in his lifetime.

Clare has been, in my view, unfairly neglected. Auden's criteria for greatness in a poet[3] offer a valid framework to demonstrate why we should read Clare's work. Firstly, Auden says a great poet must "write a lot". Clare wrote over 4,000 poems. This is both a strength and a weakness: it is difficult to find a selection which fulfils everyone's needs and interests; not all his poems are successful,[4] particularly when he tries to emulate another's style, such as 'The Parish', which is modelled on Pope, and the poems of Byron's which he rewrote in the asylum years, believing himself to be that distinguished poet revising his work. Auden admits that 'a major poet will write more bad poems than the minor'. Clare's massive output is also a strength because there is always more for a reader to discover, and there are poems to suit many different tastes.

Auden states that a major poet "must show a wide range in subject matter and treatment" with "an unmistakeable originality in vision and style". Clare writes about many things, addressing himself to the great themes of love, death and nature. Although he is a dialect poet, he stands between the worlds of literature and tradition, with a foot in both. Like Burns, that other great dialect poet, Clare has a strongly political bent and is an outspoken commentator on the evils of the day.

Arthur Symons, in his 1908 introduction to *Poems by John Clare* offers this useful comparison between Burns and Clare:

> The difference between Burns and Clare is the difference between two kinds and qualities of poetry. Burns was a great poet, filled with ideas, passions, and every sort of intoxication; but he had no such minute local lore as Clare, nor, indeed, so deep a love of the earth. He could create by naming, while Clare, who lived on the memory of his heart, had to enumerate, not leaving out one detail, because he loved every detail.[5]

Symons puts his finger on the appeal of Clare's poetry for me in the phrase "so deep a love of the earth". Throughout Clare's work, the passion feeds the eloquence, the loss and outrage. His most important poems are imbued with love and loss, they are full of heart, yet expressed with the most precise language and imagery. Clare is at his best when he is most true to himself; not when he is imitating poets he admires but when he writes what must be written, regardless of his critics, his editors, his publishers.

Clare's best poems are original and distinctive. Dialect is a contributory factor, because Clare draws on local words to good effect, such as 'clumpsing', 'progged', 'swee', 'pleachy'. He uses words like 'mouldywarp' for moles, 'pismires' for ants, 'puddocks' for buzzards. These words are vibrant, and Clare selects them deliberately. He knows Latin names for plants and animals, as evidenced in his journal, but prefers the often imaginative country names. Clare excels at close observation and startlingly original imagery, such as calling the thistle 'the very wasp of flowers' in his sonnet 'The Fear of Flowers' or his observation in 'Summer', that "reed clumps rustle like a wind shook wood".

Added to this originality is the necessary 'mastery of technique'. He takes traditional forms such as ballads and songs and bends them to his own purposes. He is inventive in his sonnets, experimenting away from the Shakespearian and Petrarchan styles, for example writing sonnets all in couplets. He tackles the long satirical poem with characteristic ambition and doggedness. Throughout his writing career he constantly evolves and improves his practice. His early work is influenced by older poets like Pope and Thomson, and dialect poets such as Bloomfield, whom he greatly admired. As he develops, his style becomes more and more distinctively his own, culminating in one of the most exquisite poems of the age, the haunting and much-anthologised 'I Am', written during the asylum years. Clare was ambitious in his writing, and, like Keats, pursued challenges and constantly tried to extend his poetry.

It is no surprise that the most passionate advocates of Clare's work have been other poets, and I can do little more than add my voice to theirs. Farley cites Michael Longley, Patrick Kavanagh and Derek Mahon as pointing the way to Clare for him. Poets Seamus Heaney and Tom Paulin have both written valuable essays on Clare, as have Matt Simpson and John Lucas. The poet David Morley's collection *The Gypsy and the Poet* (Carcanet 2013) was inspired by Clare and his friendship with Wisdom Smith, the gypsy referred to frequently in Clare's notebooks.

Clare's achievement lies in his astonishing development from the shy and solitary boy who was so inspired by reading Thomson's *The Seasons* that he felt impelled to sit on a wall on his walk home and start writing his own verses, to a mature poet writing poems no one else could have written, out of his intimate knowledge of nature and his local area, minute observation and absolute love of language. Despite his inauspicious background he established himself as a poet by sheer persistence and tenacity. He drew strongly on the oral tradition combined with literary forms and references. He was convinced of the correctness of his poetic decisions in the face of constant criticism and editing, and continued to develop his writing even though he had lost the support of the literati of the time and the approbation of those he admired. Throughout every setback, both financial and emotional, he remained devoted to his work, spending every possible moment writing poetry. He handles subjects as small as a single flower or bird's nest and as large as the broad sweep of the moors. Clare is a poet of deeply felt emotions and passions.

NOTES

1 Faber and Faber, 2007.

2 See 'Further Reading' on page 129.

3 From Auden's introduction to the anthology *Nineteenth Century British Minor Poets.*

4 According to Jonathan Bate, in the introduction to his selection of Clare poems, "He knew that he wrote too profusely and that he needed editing."

5 Published by Henry Frowde, London.

# A Country Village Year

# 1

# For pence and spicy ale

*The Shepherd's Calendar* is an ambitious poem sequence, with a lengthy section on each month. John Lucas calls it "an exuberant catalogue in which nothing is granted superiority over anything else, and the rolling catch-all syntax ... rejoices in everything that's recalled".[1] The section which describes Christmas, in 'December' is a charming introduction to the sequence. Clare is aware, even as he is writing, that the way of life he knows and loves is beginning to disappear. He is recording it for posterity in full awareness of the fact that the Industrial Revolution is changing people's lives and divorcing them from their traditions. This adds a poignant element to the poem:

> Old customs, O I love the sound
> However simple they may be:
> Whate'er wi' time has sanction found
> Is welcome and is dear to me.
> Pride grows above simplicity
> And spurns it from her haughty mind
> And soon the poet's song will be
> The only refuge they can find.

The first line of this stanza, with its soft and rounded vowels and the repeated "O", fully expresses Clare's fondness and sense of loss. The idea that pride will make people despise the simplicity of the old traditions is a shrewd one, though Clare might have been gratified to find that some elements have been preserved by those who care about the folk tradition: there are still mummers' groups today, though one has to know where to look.[2] Clare did see himself as part of this tradition; his father used to sing many of the old ballads, and Clare could play many of the old tunes on the violin.

The section on Christmas includes some uncharacteristic indoor domestic scenes. Many of Clare's poems show him alone with only nature for company. However, Christmas is a time for gathering. This poem is thronged with people visiting each other. As so often, however, the poet is an observer of others and stands outside the poem, creating a window through which the reader can watch, though not partake of, the pleasures of the season for his family and neighbours. The present tense helps to capture the sense of immediacy: "Christmas is come." The first few stanzas focus on preparations which begin with the sweeping of the house and the decoration of it with evergreens such as holly, yew and box. This all happens the day before Christmas Day, unlike the lengthy commercialised run up to Christmas that happens in today's society. The pleasures of Christmas are those of socialising and welcoming visitors, who arrive on "snow track paths" and over "rimey[3] stiles". This is a traditional English Christmas scene we recognise from Christmas cards, predating the Victorian Christmas with a decorated tree which was imported from Germany with the arrival of Prince Albert.

Although the participants are poor, Christmas is one day on which they feel rich:

> E'en want will dry its tears in mirth
> And crown him wi' a holly bough.

This personification of want (meaning need or lack) is a typical technique for the Romantic poets. Keats, for instance, personifies Melancholy, Joy, Beauty *et al*, in his beautiful odes. Clare builds in constant reminders of the work done on every other day, as "the huswife sets her spinning by" and "labour resteth from his toils." The housewife would be spinning as part of the cottage industry method of producing textiles, which was soon to be superseded by increasing mechanisation. Even Winter takes a day off and "warms his fingers", which is a lovely way of expressing the Christmas respite from the poverty and deprivation that would be experienced in the hard winters. The poet imagines Winter, like Want, as a guest at the cottager's hearths, as someone they know well, but with no occasion, for once, to harm them.

The celebrations centre on activities which change for each age group, as well as activities everyone can enjoy. The children enjoy the snow, and the festive food such as "granny's cake", and Clare describes the sound of the snow with the onomatopoeic "crumping", which beautifully evokes the packed snow underfoot. Milkmaids go for walks with their beaux to gain some privacy, and every cottage has its bunch of mistletoe, which encourages the young men to take their chance at kissing the girls, who are "giggling" in anticipation.

Music is provided by the church bells and by singers whom Clare compares to angels. This is followed by the Morris dancers who, as well as providing a lively dance, would perform the traditional mummers' play. This involved a hero, often St George or King George (hence Clare's line "the clown-turned-king", as both 'clown' and 'swain' were polite literary words for country labourers). The hero would be challenged by an enemy and there was a doctor to raise the slain back to life, symbolising the spring to come. The harlequin character is related to Punchinello, who is a hunchback and carries a bell on a stick, often with a pig's bladder blown up like a balloon, which he uses to beat people. The Punch and Judy show, much loved by children from Victorian times, is thought to be a fusion of the mummers' play and the Italian *commedia dell'arte* tradition of masked acrobats and clowns. There are certainly versions of the harlequin character all over Europe, for example in France the character is called Polichinelle; in Germany, Kasper; in Russia, Petrushka. The scripts were passed down by word of mouth and the Morris troupe would be local labourers wanting to supplement their income by providing a little entertainment. Clare's description is amusing as they "storm wi' the actor's strut and swell", which is reminiscent of the mechanicals in Shakespeare's *A Midsummer Night's Dream*, with their puffed-up star, Bottom the weaver.

Another form of local entertainment which earned "pence" for the provider was the wassail singing described in the tenth stanza of the extract. An individual or a group would tour from house to house performing Christmas carols and wassail songs, many of which are still sung today. The payment would be a bowl of spiced ale, possibly including toasted apples; and a few pennies if they could be spared. The apprentice boys join in the Christmas begging, hoping for a Christmas bonus. Clare portrays them as happy and full of energy:

> The prentice boy wi' ruddy face
> And rime-bepowdered dancing locks
> From door to door wi' happy pace
> Runs round to claim his 'Christmas box'.

The rosy-cheeked faces contrast with the frosty hair, just as in the following stanza, the blazing Christmas fires burn freely with unstinted wood, contrasting with the snowy scene outside. Again, Winter is personified as an old man, this time feeling the heat of the fire too strong and having to move away from the hearth. The fires recall spring's warmth and a cosy scene is created by Clare's descriptive details:

> While snows the winter panes bedim
> The fire curls up, a sunny charm,
> Where creaming o'er the pitcher's rim
> The flowering ale is set to warm.

"Creaming" and "flowering" are wonderful words to describe the foam at the top of the jug, and the scent of the ale, which is, of course, home-brewed and could be made from, amongst other things, hop flowers.[4] The "flowering" notion also links to Clare's references to spring, which will be the next celebratory event after Christmas, after the difficult winter months.

Clare also notices the children's activities, which remind him of his own boyhood. Some sit on their parents' knees and sing "scraps of carols" while older ones climb up on the window seats to watch the snow and:

> Likening the snow to falling feathers
> In fancy's infant ecstasy.
> Laughing wi' superstition's love
> O'er visions wild that youth supplies
> Of people pulling geese above
> And keeping Christmas in the skies.

Clare's affection for these silly little stories includes a sorrowful note that these simple pleasures are lost to him except by observing his own children and telling them stories. The fricative alliteration ("falling feathers", "fancy") and the internal pararhyme of "wild" and "supplies" combine to create a chuckling sensation, and the innocent story of the idea that geese are being plucked for Christmas dinner in heaven comes straight from the children's personal experience, as they would have seen geese being prepared for cooking. The feathers would be used to fill pillows and bedspreads.

This observation leads Clare to reminisce about his own childhood Christmases and the simple presents he used to receive on the strength of learning his lessons well: a wheeled wooden horse's head, probably home-made; gingerbread and sugared plums; picture books. Clare admits that often they only played with their toys for a little while and sometimes broke them and left them where they fell, "on the sanded floor" (which refers to the sand sprinkled on the earth floor to keep it dry). It is pleasing to recollect such memories, comments Clare, before returning to the scene before him.

This Christmas section does have a structure, albeit rather loose, since it began with Christmas preparations and the last two stanzas focus on the end of the day and the final drinks before everyone departs. People are reading their Bibles while lovers try to steal a final, secret kiss under cover of the growing gloom. The "yule cake dotted thick wi' plums" is shared alongside the stuffed chine, which is a dish made with pork backbone and stuffed with herbs. Both these luxurious foodstuffs were made in advance and left to mature, as was the elderberry wine offered to guests for a final toast. Country people were skilled foragers and nothing would go to waste, as we see in 'Sport in the Meadows' when people are gathering cowslips for both tea and wine. Both elderflowers and elderberries were used to make wine and other beverages relatively cheaply.

The rambling structure of this poem allows Clare to wander off into his own recollections and musings, which keep the reader interested and take the poem beyond the descriptive. The lively scenes contrast with Clare's quiet reflections, just as the warm fire contrasts with the snow outside. The iambic tetrameters[5] and the alternate rhyme scheme help to keep the poem's energy moving forward and prove a flexible medium for Clare's range of tone in this charming poem. In a way, it helps to set the context for the rest of the Everyman selection, as here readers can see for themselves the way of life about to be destroyed for ever. Clare is not a poet to prettify rural life, but here he allows himself to create a glow of happiness. Christmas is a respite for the workers and a time to share the bounty they have saved up during the rest of the year. It is a time for community and entertainment.

NOTES

1 *John Clare* by John Lucas (Northcote House, 1994).

2 Often to be found in rural villages and performing at local events around Christmastime.

3 Ice formed by freezing fog as the droplets of moisture fall on exposed objects.

4 Ale and beer were not always interchangeable terms. It is possible that the ale Clare is speaking of here did not include hop flowers.

5 A tetrameter is a line of four metrical feet; in this case they are iambic feet, which have a pattern of an unstressed syllable followed by a stressed one.

## 2

# He plods about his toils

The second stanza of Keats' much-loved ode 'To Autumn' is a fine example of the picturesque descriptions of nature which were part of the Romantic vision. Keats' 'Autumn' is personified as a rather lazy figure who relaxes and does very little work:

> Who hath not seen thee oft amid thy store?
>  Sometimes whoever seeks abroad may find
> Thee sitting careless on a granary floor,
>  Thy hair soft-lifted by the winnowing wind;
> Or on a half-reap'd furrow sound asleep,
>  Drows'd with the fume of poppies, while thy hook
>  Spares the next swath and all its twined flowers:
> And sometimes like a gleaner thou dost keep
>  Steady thy laden head across a brook;
>  Or by a cyder-press, with patient look,
>  Thou watchest the last oozings hours by hours.

Clare, however, is not a city boy like Keats. From the age of seven he was labouring in the fields to bring in some much-needed income for his family. He was lucky to attend school until he was twelve; however, his attendance was sporadic, being kept at home to work during busy times. Jonathan Bate describes July as "a month of backbreaking labour in the fields".[1] Clare sees the countryside is as a workplace for himself and others, whereas for Keats, it was a place where he went for holidays, away from the bustling cities. There are many Clare poems which show workers going about their duties: milkmaids, shepherds, bird boys and the rest. There is a sense of purpose about many of the characters he includes, far from the sense of drowsiness in Keats' poem. In 'To Autumn', Keats was saying goodbye for ever to the English countryside, as he was about to travel south for his health.[2] However, like Keats, Clare is often an observer. He liked spending time alone, reading or writing, and would creep away from work if the need to write overwhelmed him. In his own words: "I used to drop down behind a hedge bush or dyke and write down my things upon the crown of my hat."[3] The poems which focus on this theme in the Everyman edition are: 'The barn door is open', 'The Wheat Ripening', 'The maiden ran away', 'She tied up her few things', 'The Foddering Boy', 'Winter Fields'. Clare gives us an idea of how difficult yet full of compensations the labourer's life was.

'The barn door is open' captures a moment in the middle of the day in late summer. Written in the present tense and rhyming couplets, the latter unusual for a sonnet, it offers a tableau of what both people and animals are doing at that precise moment:

> The woodman is resting and getting his dinner …
> And cows in the pasture all feeding together.

The sense of immediacy is further enhanced by the many present participles Clare includes, such as "resting", "drinking", "a-making", "a-feeding", "a-noising". The profusion of verbs in this poem indicates how busy the scene is. Everyone works at their own tasks to bring in the harvest. Both "the mower" and "the maid" are working in the fields while the woodman rests. Instead of presenting a series of beautiful still images, as Keats does, Clare's observation takes the reader's eyes on a panoramic vision of one busy moment, a snapshot of country life.

"The Wheat Ripening" with its alternate rhyme scheme, is a happy sonnet. It presents field work as a pleasant spectacle, and shows man in harmony with nature. The milkmaid sings ("Making life light with song") and the shepherd whistles, the ploughman utters "cheering calls" and the birdboy's[4] calls mingle with the song of the lark. It is a poem full of sounds and colours, all harmonious to the early-morning walker on the "footpath's narrow way". Clare rejoices in the beauty to be seen as he walks on the narrow strips of grass dividing the fields – or 'balk'.

It is closer to the beauty of the Keats poem but seen from the standpoint of one used to country ways. Contrasts are achieved by the way the colours are described; wheat is "rusty brown" and "barley bleaches". Dewdrops are "glittering" and "sparkling". There is a more peaceful mood than in 'The barn door is open' because it is the early morning, unpeopled until the sixth line when the milkmaid sets off for work, singing as she goes. The last few lines are full of activity as the ploughman and the shepherd begin their day's work. Clare is a lone observer, as he so often is, remarking only that "it is sweet". Keats shows us autumn exquisitely through the eyes of an outsider. Clare gives us insider knowledge.

Another sonnet, 'The maiden ran away' is a delightful evocation of what heavy rain does to the countryside and its people. It is a serious rainstorm, so heavy that the women "scream" and a deep pit is filled to the top. The delight is in the detail:

> The maiden ran away to fetch the clothes
> And threw her apron o'er her cap and bows
> But the shower catched her ere she hurried in
> And beat and almost dowsed her to the skin.

This is a beautifully observed scene which is still familiar today. Clare chooses strong verbs so that the rain's force is captured and dramatised. Everyone is caught out and hurries home, and even "the birds are almost drowned upon the trees".

'Winter Fields' is a further poem where the weather causes suffering but gives the poet an interesting topic. The "striding shepherd" has a strong sense of purpose as he goes to see the depth of water that floods the path. However, the sense of hardship also comes across as the man is "shouldering onward" as though fighting the wind, and the dog is "loath" to follow him, "croodling",[5] snuggling against his master. In the last line, the dog "hirkles through", looking for the best path, jumping over puddles. The cold and damp permeate the sonnet itself; the fields are "mire and sludge", very tactile words, and the paths are "pudgy", that is, full of puddles. The plosive alliteration combined with the internal pararhyme of "sludge" and "pudgy" helps to create a sense of sticky unpleasant mud. Clare's choice of dialect words throughout his work makes his writing gritty and down to earth, as well as adding to his uniqueness. Clare's Northamptonshire voice is distinctive and belongs to its own region, just as Bloomfield's native Suffolk and Burns' native Scotland furnished their work with its own unique stamp.

'She tied up her few things' tells of the life of an itinerant worker, in this case a girl, Jinney. It is a compassionate vignette describing first the preparations she makes to leave town, then the manner of her leaving and finally how the flowers will miss her next year. The list of her meagre belongings illustrates her poverty, without a trace of pity. Her bonnet is "worn through at the crown" and her most treasured possession is a Bible. It is time to move on as the work is done for the year and she must return home. She senses this rather than being told to move on, or perhaps she is anxious about her family. The marking of the page in the Bible suggests turning over to a new phase, or marking a particular verse she needs. The first stanza is full of verbs such as "laced", and "tied" and "lapped up"[6] which indicate finality, and the touching detail of the cleanliness of her caps shows she takes great pride in herself. Only one person says goodbye to her as she slips away: the thresher working in the barn who wishes her good luck. However, the dog licks her hand and the horse lets her pass, while the other farmyard and wild animals fill the scene with noise and activity. The first and last stanza focus on her, while the middle section shows the activities of others, indicating that she does not figure strongly and life there goes on. Only the spring flowers will miss her. The last line offers comfort as "ere the sun's set'll be in her own town". The form is an interesting one, because each stanza has short rhyming couplets interspersed with longer lines after the second and fourth lines. This gives a song-like effect with clustering rhymes and a dying fall in the longer lines, an excellent way of creating contrast through prosody.

'The Foddering Boy', like 'She tied up her few things' focuses on one individual who stands for the many. In 1924, the poem was criticised by Edmund Gosse as "lacking … the intellectual element of Wordsworth. Every detail which photography can seize is precisely rendered, but all is exterior; there is not a phrase that shows the poet 'transfusing' himself into the life of the Foddering Boy."[7] However, as in 'She tied up her few things', the empathy is in the detail. The boy has "straw-band-belted legs" and "folded arm", "beats his fingers warm" and shakes the "lodging snows from off his clothes". Clare's approach to his subject may be closer to the modern sensibility. As William Howard notes, in his book *John Clare* (1981),[8] "there is no didactic intrusion by the poet; we sense his sympathetic response to what he sees." There is no need for Clare to become the foddering boy; he knew only too well what it was like to carry out such tasks in bad weather. By removing the persona, he omits any trace of patronising pity for the boy, whose sole concern is to feed the cows without allowing the cold to penetrate his clothes. The poem takes the Shakespearian sonnet form[9] with the ending rhyming couplet bringing a sense of accomplishment that the job is done:

> He litters the sweet hay about the ground
> And brawls to call the staring cattle round.

The cattle are depending on him: "expecting cattle … impatient for the sound", just as the cows in their turn are depended on, showing the harmony between man and nature in the ancient farming methods. The poem needs no moral pointing out. A review of *The Rural Muse*, in *Blackwood Magazine*, called Clare "the poet of the poor" and added this:

> His sympathies, his enjoyments, his habits, and aspirations, are all those of the poor man. Despised as the poor are in England, they who despise them cannot rob them of their intellectual pleasures – of their purer sensations – of fair Nature's light. The poor then must look to their own poets. A mite[10] from them might place Clare where he ought to be, and enable him to continue to delight them, and the wise and feeling of every rank, with his simple and touching verse …[11]

This is a fair summary of what Clare gives the reader when he writes about the country as a workplace. He is both one of his fellows and slightly apart from them, being a sensitive and thoughtful man who loved solitude and books. He experienced working life for himself and allows the reader to understand what it was like to be a rural labourer in the nineteenth century. He does it in such a way as to delight the senses while recreating life as it was, not as nostalgia would make it.

NOTES

1 *John Clare: A Biography* (Picador, 2003).

2 Keats was to die abroad, and at the time of writing this poem, he knew he had tuberculosis.

3 *John Clare by Himself*, edited by Eric Robinson and David Powell (Carcanet, 1996).

4 A bird boy's job was to scare the birds away from the crops.

5 "To cower or crouch down; to draw oneself together, as for warmth; to cling close together, or nestle close to a person" (*OED*).

6 'Lapped' is a dialect form of the word 'wrapped'.

7 *Clare: The Critical Heritage*, edited by Mark Storey (Routledge, 1973).

8 Twayne Publishers, Boston, 1981.

9 Three quatrains and a rhyming couplet, which encapsulates a 'turn' in the argument.

10 Meaning 'a little', 'a small amount'.

11 Quoted in *Clare: The Critical Heritage.*

# 3

## A picture to the place

“My mother said that I never should/Play with the gypsies in the wood” goes the old skipping rhyme. This sums up the distrust that ‘respectable’ people felt towards these travellers. Jonathan Bate, Clare’s most recent biographer, confirms that the society of the time held them in deep distrust: they were “demonised not only for their begging and pilfering, but also because their strange language was suggestive of the black arts”.[1] Like the Jews (see, for example ‘The Ballad of Little Sir Hugh’), they were thought to be guilty of child murder.

As a solitary wanderer in his leisure time, however, Clare would naturally happen upon gypsy encampments. He came to befriend and visit the gypsies in the area, partly attracted by the beautiful Romany women. While Clare envied the travellers their freedom, he knew himself too well to imagine that he could ever join them, rooted as he was to Helpston. However, they did provide a source of inspiration for him. He learned many tunes from them, which he wrote down, thus making a significant contribution to the preservation of traditional music. In his own words: “Got the tune of ‘Highland Mary’ from Wisdom Smith, a gipsy, and pricked another sweet tune without a name as he fiddled it.”[2] Clare loved music and draws on it frequently in his adopting of musical forms such as ballads and songs. He learned many of the old ballads from his father.

Clare’s interest in the gypsies was ambivalent. As Ronald Blythe puts it in his interesting essay on ‘Clare and the Gypsies’: “He both hobnobbed with them and was fastidious where they were concerned, was prejudiced and unprejudiced at the same time. He wrote many poems about them which envied their lot, their freedom, their women, and one poem which envied them nothing.”[3] The one he refers to in the latter part of this comment is ‘The Gypsy Camp’, the only poem about the gypsies included in the Everyman selection. It describes a gypsy encampment in winter, and is in sonnet form. The first line emphasises the isolation of the camp and the extremely cold weather: “The snow falls deep; the Forest lies alone." The caesura[4] slows down the line and creates an atmosphere of secrecy, an idea developed later in the poem by the concealed camp "half hid in snow". The effort of the humans to keep warm arouses our sympathy; as Blythe says, there is no trace of envy in this poem: "The Gypsy knocks his hands and tucks them up." Words like "squalid", "stinking" and "hovel" show Clare's revulsion for their lifestyle. At the same time, he admires the cleverness of their survival strategies such as making camp where an oak tree can act as a windbreak, and using the snow to provide cover. The binary oppositions of opposing temperatures provide contrasts: "snow" and "wind" create a sense of chill, yet "fire", "roasts", "half-roasted dog" and "heat" offset that coldness by focusing the reader's attention on the fire which is central to the camp and to the survival of the vagabonds. Gypsies did not live in caravans at that time, but would make tents from willow to provide winter shelter.

Clare's fellow-feeling for animals, a constant throughout his work, draws the reader's eyes to the dog, which is waiting intently to see if anyone will spare a little food. No one does. This detail allows readers to see for themselves how scarce food is and how poor the gypsies are, so that when we reach the penultimate line, we see the reason for their "pilfering" and do not judge them. They are "unprotected" and gain no support from society. The dog's experience indicates the unbearably strong heat of the campfire, so that one has to move away after a while; one is either too hot or too cold. This also applies to humans, but by foregrounding the dog's difficulties Clare shows the reader how society views the gypsies. We can see how the gypsies in their turn are ignored by society, just as they ignore the dog, considering its needs less important than their own. There is no moral judgement made. Clare is telling the reader how things are.

The sonnet is unrhymed until the concluding couplet, which acts as a summary of Clare's feelings, a comment on the vagabond way of life, but also a drawing back, a de-briefing, a return to 'civilisation', compared to the blunt and comfortless unrhymed twelve lines which precede it. The couplet has a summarising function as well as drawing out the comparison between the dog and the gypsies:

> 'Tis thus they live, a picture to the place:
> A quiet, pilfering, unprotected race.

The one negative word, "pilfering", has been set into context by Clare's poem. The reader sees that stealing is necessary to survival, and Clare softens the thieving by choosing a gentle word which means to steal small items of little value, taking things which their owners will not miss. Lacking support, they have to resort to dishonesty. But they repay people by being "quiet" and a "picture to the place". Clare sees them almost as wild animals, going unobtrusively about the business of survival.

The influence of the gypsies on Clare's work extends far beyond his writing about them. The enclosures which so distressed him also made their lives more difficult, because they made the common lands their home and their means of survival. He saw them as friends and fellow roamers (although their roaming was much wider than his). He contacted local gypsies for help when he was in Dr Allen's private asylum. These were the particular ones that inspired this sonnet. Bate says that Clare discovered them by accident while walking in Epping Forest in winter. He was permitted some liberty while he was at this private asylum, which is what enabled him to leave of his own accord and walk home to Helpston, in his famous freedom walk.[5]

NOTES

1 *John Clare: A Biography*, by Jonathan Bate (Picador, 2003).

3 *John Clare by Himself*, edited by Eric Robinson and David Powell (Carcanet, 1996).

3 'Vagabondage in a Native Place: John Clare and the Gypsies'.

4 Caesura: a deliberate pause in the middle (or thereabouts) of the line.

5 It is much documented that Clare walked from Epping Forest back to Helpston, sleeping rough and begging for food. See chapter 18 for a fuller discussion of his mental breakdown and its consequences.

# 4

# Happy to be poor

Clare is an excellent observer of people and held strong values about what he admired. Some of his portraits of people are affectionate, others less so. He writes about character types rather than people he knew personally, which allows him licence to express his views. In 'The Cottager', he presents a character who is contented with his lot, whereas in 'The Parish' extract, he expresses his disapproval of social climbers in a far more satiric tone.

'The Cottager' is an affectionate, slightly satirical portrait of the type of old man Clare would be familiar with, someone who has never travelled far from the village and lives a narrow but happy existence, content with his lot. Like many old people, he is set in his ways and holds strong opinions. The poem is reminiscent of the character portraits in Chaucer's Prologue to *The Canterbury Tales*, especially as, like Chaucer, Clare sustains the poem with rhyming couplets and iambic pentameter.

The old man is predictable in his habits, expressed in the simile "true as the church clock". This is witty because not only does it imply the man is religious, it also illustrates his slow ponderousness. He "plods" rather than walks, and can stand for an hour chatting at the blacksmith's. He has little experience of any other sort of life and is "twenty years" behind the times. He has been content never to visit "Lunon" (London) in his whole life; unlike Clare, who may have wished at times that he had never done so. Visiting London and becoming part of its literary 'scene' was both Clare's dream and his undoing. This taste of fame disassociated him from the contentment of his everyday life; his subsequent neglect as a poet may have contributed to his depression. The old man described in this poem could have been based on many old men that Clare knew, including his own father, Parker Clare, but it could also have been the outcome of Clare's own life, had he not fallen in love with making poetry.

The cottager's attitude to modern inventions is amusing: he regards them as "witchcraft" and "blasphemy", though there were many like him who regarded the railway as dangerous, especially since the death of

William Huskisson MP, killed by Stephenson's *Rocket* engine in 1830, the same year the poem was written, not to mention the earlier deaths of less well-known persons in 1821 and 1828 in collisions with trains.

The cottager is a simple man, elevated from some of his contemporaries as he can read: "Still neighbours prize him as the learned man." The irony here is that he is only "learned" in the village context. He cannot always understand the new vicar's sermons, and "shakes his head ... such mighty learning meets his ears/He thinks it Greek or Latin which he hears." He is strenuously behind the times and proud of it. He "reads the news" but seems to take delight in disapproving. He also reads the Bible, prayer book and other works on a religious theme. The reading of religious books was encouraged in the poor at that time. The one poet he likes is Tusser (1524–80), an English poet who was a farmer. Tusser wrote *A Hundreth Good Pointes of Husbandrie*, a long poem in rhyming couplets recording the country year, which is not dissimilar to the idea behind Clare's *The Shepherd's Calendar*, a project which was suggested to Clare by his publisher (also Keats'), John Taylor. Tusser is a good choice for such a character: safe, pious and sufficiently old-fashioned. He comes from the same part of the country as Clare, living around Cambridge and Essex. Most poetry is too fanciful for the cottager – another reason Tusser is a good fit. Like Clare's own father, the cottager can recite old ballads from memory and performs these party tricks at Christmas.

The cottager is a family man who treasures reminders of his children, such as the pretty snail shells they collected. He delights in telling stories from his own boyhood, which was a happy one spent roaming free in the surrounding countryside "on rapture's easy wing". His pictures are decorated with ears of corn, and the treasured prints themselves illustrate his national pride: they are of British military and naval heroes: John Manners, Marquis of Granby (1721–70) and Lord Rodney (1719–92).

The cottager's one-roomed home is "spare" in the sense that he owns very little. He is drying beans on strings hanging from the rafters and his small "library" is kept in an "old corner cupboard". However, the hovel is in a sheltered spot: "He hears the mountain storm and feels it not." He has no worries, and time itself does not concern him as he has barely noticed turning grey. He lives for the moment and his memories, never worrying about the future. Like the "mountain storm", unhappiness and anxiety do not touch him.

Admittedly, this is a rather romanticised pen portrait, and there is a sense of wistfulness in it, as though Clare might envy the contentment of the cottager; but equally there must have been people like this, unaffected by life's storms and existing in blissful ignorance of what else life could offer, particularly before the enclosures robbed country people of their right to roam, increasing their hardships. They were no longer able to forage for food and fuel in the common lands, since they were fenced off and guarded.

'The Parish' is an ambitious poem. As he indicates in his epigraph, Clare is following Pope's 'An Epistle to Dr Arbuthnot'. Pope's work is an attack on flatterers, and Clare similarly disapproves of falseness. The character types who are satirised in Clare's poem are all people who put on false airs, making themselves ridiculous. As in 'The Cottager', one of its main themes is poverty. Clare harks back to the good old days when farmers used to treat the poor well and as equals:

> That good old fame the farmers earned of yore,
> That made as equals, not as slaves, the poor,
> That good old fame did in two sparks expire:
> A shooting coxcomb and a hunting Squire;
> And their old mansions that was dignified
> With things far better than the pomp of pride,
> At whose oak table that was plainly spread
> Each guest was welcomed and the poor was fed;
> Where master, son and serving-man and clown
> Without distinction daily sat them down;
> Where the bright rows of pewter by the wall
> Served all the pomp of kitchen or of hall;
> These all have vanished like a dream of good
> And the slim things that rises where they stood
> Are built by those whose clownish taste aspires
> To hate their farms and ape the country squires.

Clare's language creates a cheery atmosphere with the "bright rows of pewter" and the "oak table" in contrast to the "slim" modern reality, which sounds mean and dull. The farmers are criticised for their new tastes now that pride has overtaken generosity. The plosive alliteration in "pomp of pride" expresses this forcefully.

He also holds up for ridicule the farmers' daughters who have put on airs and graces, "taught at school their stations to despise", and who no longer preserve the old customs. Formerly they had rosy cheeks but now they are "shrouded in veils green", which makes them sound ill and deathly pale. They aspire to achieve the status of the accomplished woman,[1] but this is inappropriate for farmers' daughters. Clare views them as attempting to join a society they were not born into and not suited to, and making themselves unhappy by so doing:

> Prim as the pasteboard figures which they cut
> At school and tasteful on the chimney put,
> They sit before their glasses hour by hour
> Or paint unnatural daubs of fruit or flower,
> Or, boasting learning, novels' beauties quotes
> Or, aping fashion, scream a tune by notes.

We are left in no doubt of Clare's opinion of their art work because of his negative lexical choices "unnatural daubs" and their vanity in sitting "hour by hour" before their mirrors. Clare did not pursue a relationship with Mary Joyce because he imagined she was socially his superior, so there is a personal note of bitterness behind this satire. Mary Joyce's feelings and behaviour are not known. Clare is more likely railing against the aspirations of those hoping to rise socially by aping the behaviour of the aristocracy and *nouveaux riches.* He himself had social aspirations from his poetry, but it is the lack of being oneself he seems most to despise here.

The extract concludes with two particular stories: one about "Miss Peevish Scornful" who sets her cap at a young squire but ends up running away with his servant because she fears she will be left on the shelf. Her pride is humbled. The other story is Young Farmer Bigg, who becomes a wicked seducer of young girls. He is effeminate and even wears a corset. Although some people talk about him and point him out as wicked, his friends are loyal to him. This is not a cautionary tale, but a story of someone who is corrupted by his upward mobility. Clare's point in these two poems is that if you are true to yourself, you will be contented, like the cottager; but if you try to be what you are not, you will bring ruin upon yourself. These are simple ideas, but expressed in an entertaining and readable way. Perhaps too, these poems pave the way for Clare's increasingly political stance on the oppression of the poor and the part the land enclosures played in it.

NOTES

1 As discussed in Jane Austen novels such as *Pride and Prejudice*, where women wanting to marry well had to draw, paint, be fashionable, speak French, sing and play musical instruments, embroider and so on.

# 5

# The fireside evening

In 'Winter Fields', Clare calls for a book "to cheat the sway/Of Winter". The cottager enjoys reading his Bible by the fireside. But in 'St Martin's Eve', Clare describes a less solitary winter entertainment, a party. He opens the poem with three stanzas evoking the cold and misery of winter, so that he can go on to draw a contrast between the miserable days and the fun of socialising in the evening. St Martin's Day was 11th November, so the evening party would happen on the 10th. Traditionally people began fasting on St Martin's day. St Martin's Eve, like Shrove Tuesday before Lent,[1] was a last chance to feast and enjoy oneself, before beginning a period of forty days when the diet will be frugal and plain. There are practical reasons for this fasting as food may be in short supply, as well as religious ones of seeking purity. This period became what we now call Advent, but it is now shorter.

It was the time of year that the work of harvesting was completed and casual workers, like the girl in 'She tied up her few things', would leave and go to the hiring fair to gain a new position. Hiring fairs were held all over the country during Martinmas week. Employers would choose their workers for next year and seal the deal with a small payment. There are many folk songs which document the tradition, often linked to the theme of unrequited love. The stalls and entertainment which grew up around these fairs would have provided a much-needed income for traders and a last enjoyment before winter made such occasions difficult.

The first three stanzas offer a bleak presentation of the miseries of November. Clare deplores the over-long nights and the short days, the lack of activity for young people who cannot play in the fields and indulge in summer pastimes like those described in 'Sport in the Meadows'. Children are trapped indoors by the rain and cannot roam outside searching for "wild fruit". In crowded cottages like the one Clare lived in with his wife, children and his aged parents, this must have been a hardship. He calls it "Winter's imprisonment". Likewise, the joys of nature have gone for another year, many of his favourite birds have migrated, and he misses the marten and the swallow. The worst thing for Clare is that the birdsong is silenced: "the woods are desolate of song". The crane's call sounds to him "melancholy … like a traveller lost". Instead of the "busy tribes" of birds, the features of the landscape cloud and "enshroud" the sky. The verb "enshroud" evokes death, developing the idea from the opening line of the year being "wearisome with age". There are also winds and floods which can devastate the landscape and spoil its beauty. These miserable conditions drive people indoors and the attractions of the fireside are all they have for comfort. According to Clare, the activities of telling stories and drinking wine, made from wild fruits such as elderberries, are popular at such gatherings of friends.

Having set the party into context, Clare moves into specifics. The poet is an observer at the St Martin's Eve party he describes. It is a very noisy party: "the old cottage rung with merriment". The weather outside serves to make the event cosier. A musical metaphor for the wind, "blustering howl of outdoor symphonies", is typical of Clare, his love for nature coming through even when it is unpleasant. The fare is traditional: roasted apples, home-made ale and nutmeg toast, a simple and inexpensive supper. Little domestic details, like "the glad cat" who is enjoying curling up in the warmth, enhance the scene. The entertainment is all home-made too, and seems crude and unsophisticated to modern eyes, as the company delights in playing practical jokes on one another. One participant opens his mouth for a surprise, thinking to receive a sweetmeat, but is given a mouthful of ashes. Another has his finger bitten by someone who challenges him to place a finger on the wall on a "pretended mark" while blindfolded. These and other silly tricks amuse the gathered company who howl with laughter at the person duped.

In the midst of all this jollity, Clare points out a lonely figure, Kate, who remains aloof. He tells us the reason: that she "made one slip in love and played the fool". Clare suggests that she is fated to remain single, but she herself has not given up hope, and that night plans to place a red onion under her pillow so that she will dream of the one she will marry. This is a custom more often associated with St Thomas' Eve. Clare's inclusion of it here may reflect a local superstition. The two stanzas about Kate create a moment of still melancholy to contrast with the japes of the unthinking guests. Instead of dancing she "sits behind" in a thoughtful posture: "her pallid cheek upon her hand reclined". The word 'pallid' suggests her sadness is making her unwell. Ironically, depression is preventing her from attracting a mate.

The music is all home-made, using such simple instruments as the comb and paper, and an improvised drum: "one thumps the warming pan with merry glee". Clare was an accomplished fiddle-player, but he values the innocence of these people who can "fancy music in such clamorous noise". He expresses the idea that it is not the quality that matters but how it is perceived:

> Like those converting all they touch to gold
> These all they hearken to convert to joys.

After the dancing, people settle down to hear stories "often read yet never stale". Clare jokes that they believe them because they are set down in a book, but goes on to summarise the stories with affection, enjoying the reactions of the audience:

> Bluebeard and all his murders' dread parade
> Are listened to and mourned for and the tear
> Drops from the blue eye of the listening maid,
> Warm as it fell upon her lover's bier.

The tale of Tibb, the tinker's daughter, is given a more detailed treatment because it is less well known. The story has many twists and turns but falls into the rags-to-riches genre, and it would of course be very appealing to the audience, to see a lowly tinker's daughter join the ranks of the aristocracy.

The concluding stanza includes some lovely imagery as the party breaks up at midnight:

> To seek their cottages they tittering go:
> Heartened with sports and stout ale berry-brown,
> Beside their dames like Chanticleer they crow
> While every lanthorn flings long gleams along the snow.

Chanticleer is the name of the cockerel in Chaucer's *Canterbury Tales*, which in turn was based on folk story. This simile provides a link to traditional stories like those shared at the party, and suggests that the men are laughing raucously, like cocks crowing. They are still mentally in the creative landscape of the stories, imagining themselves to be characters within them. The last line summons up a vivid scene of the lantern swinging from the hands of the home-goers, its light casting moving beams of light as their walking gathers pace.

Clare maintains a complex stanza form throughout the poem, which gives it coherence and holds the readers' interest. The intricate rhyme scheme of *a b a b b c b c c* is employed throughout and is kept subtle by extensive enjambment. Clare's iambic pentameters offer a driving pace and contribute to the sense of tautness. Clare's accomplishment in this apparently straightforward poem is impressive.

NOTES

1 Shrove Tuesday is the eve of Ash Wednesday. Both Advent and Lent are significant periods of prayer before major Christian festivals, Christmas and Easter respectively.

# 6

# The landscape laughs in Spring

Spring is an important time in the rural calendar. There is much work to be done in preparing fields and planting crops. The season is full of joy because the weather has improved and life is easier, after the privations of winter, but there is also a 'hungry gap' because no new crops are ready to eat and only the crops which have overwintered are available for food. However, children can play out of doors again, thus relieving the feeling of overcrowding in the cramped cottages.

In the Everyman selection, there are two poems in particular which celebrate the exuberance of the season. 'Sport in the Meadows', a happy account of how children pass their time in innocent pleasure, is strongly reminiscent of Blake's *Songs of Innocence*,[1] in particular 'The Ecchoing Green' where the children are playing and older people watch them indulgently. 'The Landscape laughs in Spring' is remarkably congruent with Blake's poem 'Laughing Song' from *Songs of Innocence*, with the same pathetic fallacy[2] of a joyous landscape:

> When the green woods laugh with the voice of joy,
> And the dimpling stream runs laughing by;

which compares to Clare's lines:

> The landscape laughs in Spring and stretches on
> Its growing distance of refreshing dyes.

Both poets have used personification to good effect here, and see the landscape as actively rejoicing. Blake illustrates the concept of innocence in his poems, but Clare displays the pleasure he feels in the reawakening of nature. Both are firmly rooted in the Romantic tradition of freedom and a love of the natural world. Blake draws on very similar things to Clare, but uses them to different ends.

Both 'Sport in the Meadows' and 'The landscape laughs in Spring' are accomplished poems. 'Sport in the Meadows' is a headlong rush of alternately rhymed iambic pentameters in one long stanza, a form well suited to the expression of the children's energy and delight as they rush about collecting cowslips. Each quatrain is in alternate rhyme, providing harmony and variety. The poem is full of action and high spirits. The run-on lines[3] help to express the movement of the children as they play. They play with things which nature provides, such as a ball made from flowers (a cuckaball) and rush about looking for birds' nests and cowslips to pick. Even the animals seem to join in the fun as they too want the cowslips:

> The sheep and cows are crowding for a share
> And snatch the blossoms in such eager haste
> That basket-bearing children running there
> Do think within their hearts they'll get them all
> And hoot and drive them from their graceless waste

This creates a comical scene as the children and animals are in competition for these golden flowers of early spring. The children feel that the animals "waste" the flowers by eating them, but they want them to make a ball with to throw to each other, which is much more wasteful. The children are also gathering them for sustenance: "For they want some for tea and some for wine".

Tea made from cowslip flowers by infusing them in boiling water was used for medicinal purposes. It is a good diuretic and is useful for headaches. Country people make wine from many wild flowers and berries, another activity which was curtailed somewhat by the enclosures. In 'The landscape laughs in Spring', Clare refers to cowslip tea and cowslip wine, using a beautiful metaphor:

> To make praise-worthy wine and savoury tea,
> And drink a Winter memory of May
> When all the season's joys have ceased to be
> And flowers and sunny hours have passed away.

The wine is a comfort in winter: it preserves the warmth of spring in its flavour and sweetness. Cowslip wine is usually sweet and rich, a dessert wine.

'Sport in the Meadows' begins with a picturesque description of a meadow in May, when the cowslip "peeps" (or first buds) have grown into large golden flowers, and the fields are full of other spring plants such as:

"water-blobs", the local name for marsh marigolds; lady-smocks, which are white or pale blue; daisies and buttercups. Clare describes all these wildflowers as "shining here and there", a lovely visual metaphor which suggests they appear in the fields like stars against the night sky, bright and glowing. He says the marsh marigolds, which grow in damp conditions, and "crowd" by the bridge ('brig' is a dialect word for bridge), and compares the spread of plants to "morts of folken flocking at a fair" with delicate alliteration, assonance and consonance. A fair is a merry occasion, something country folk look forward to, so this metaphor suits the atmosphere and allows readers to identify with the spring flowers.

The poem is full of verbs: "snatch", "hoot", "drive", "shout", and the middle section in particular echoes with noise and hubbub. By constructing loose-limbed sentences tagged together with dashes, Clare creates a sense of rush and joy. There's a tale of a girl who drops her basket and spills all her blossoms, and another who loses her bonnet to the wind. The children help each other, adding to the happy impression. Clare refers to a child standing on a molehill to reach for a "bunch of May". May is the blossom of the hawthorn tree; it has a strong musky smell and small white flowers with pink centres. Some think it unlucky to bring it into the house. It is what is referred to in the old rhyme that advises the listener, "Ne'er cast a clout/till May be out."[4] The thorns scratch the child, but plantain leaves are used to soothe it. This is not the plantain used in Caribbean cookery but a common British weed, *Plantago major,* whose broad leaves were used to soothe inflamed skin, or rubbed fresh on stings to bring pain relief. These children are fully versed in country remedies. The poem concludes with the animals running away from the noisy children, "marauders" who return every day. The "noising childern" also feature in 'The landscape laughs in Spring' in a cameo appearance for a few lines.

'The landscape laughs in Spring' is also in iambic pentameter, but this time is a sonnet in the Petrarchan style, with an alternate rhyme scheme but no division of octet and sestet. Rather than concentrating mostly on one aspect, it gives a taut panorama of all the activities that are going on in nature, like an aerial view of the country. "Pewit-haunted flats" suggests the darker notes of winter, in the word "haunted", but now the floods have dispersed and the meadows are full of flowers. The lines:

> The trickling brook veins sparkling to the sun
> Like to young may-flies dancing wi' the hours

are not only beautifully observed but contain a hint that this pleasure is short-lived, as mayflies live only briefly, from a few hours to a few days. Clare's feelings towards spring are full of pleasure, made the more intense because it cannot last. This idea is emphasised by the concluding three lines quoted above, which lament the passing of the 'flowers and sunny hours' with an internal rhyme.

These two spring poems are delightful. They are full of the precise observations that Clare is admired for. He follows through with his poems about summer, which are also rich with detail, but lack the exuberance of these spring poems.

NOTES

1 1789.

2 A literary device in which an inanimate object is given human feelings.

3 Enjambment.

4 Many people today think this refers to the month of May. The hawthorn does not bloom until the weather is sufficiently clement, so that wearing extra clothing is not necessary.

# 7

# Summer's mellowing pencil

There are four poems in the Everyman selection which focus particularly on summer. They are all sonnets: 'The Wheat Ripening', 'The Beans in Blossom', 'Summer Tints' and 'Summer Moods'. They all have themes in common which are characteristic of Clare: flora and fauna; the countryside as a place of work; the crops; the beauty of nature; solitude. Clare is always an observer, never a worker, in these poems. As discussed in Chapter 2, Clare does not see the natural world as a place of pastoral fantasy but a place where people work.[1] However, the labour does not detract from the landscape, but adds to its loveliness. Clare enjoys the changes each season brings to the familiar fields. Nature is for him eternally renewing itself and sustaining the country people.

In 'The Wheat Ripening', the colours of the wheat field are "rusty brown" in contrast with the barley's "mellow gray". These are the shades of the early morning, whereas in 'Summer Moods' Clare shows us "eventide". The absence of colour in this sonnet indicates that he is walking in twilight. There is just enough light to see the snails which are coming out from the long grass. Sounds and perfumes are heightened: the "sad and weary drone" of the bees helps to set the quiet mood. The bees are lamenting for flowers which were so recently in bloom but now are gone. Summer's beauty is transient. The calls of the quail and the landrail (sometimes called the corncrake) add to the peacefulness of the moment; "wet my foot" and "craik craik" are the verbal representations of their cries. Both birds are notoriously difficult to see, and the poet only hears them, knows that they are there, concealed in the grass. Clare's description of the landrail as "fairylike" gives the poem a sense of magic and wonder as does the lovely simile "hid as thoughts unborn". The scent of mown grass permeates the evening, and by the end of the poem the light has gone, evening wears a "dewy veil" and light fades into "glooms". Clare has a gift for catching and preserving a moment. He was criticised for being descriptive by his publisher and editor, John Taylor: "I have often remarked that your Poetry is much the best when you are not describing common Things ..."[2] The lack of the philosophising

Taylor demands is precisely what endears Clare to the modern reader. The taste for philosophical works in poetry has abated somewhat, and Clare's tightly made observational poems are much more to the modern taste.

If 'Summer Moods' is beautifully reflective, 'The Wheat Ripening', on the other hand, is full of brio, created by the many present participles: glittering, sparkling, journeying, milking, grazing, ploughing, cheering, whistling, unceasing. It is early morning and the fields are full of workers, all busy, while the poet is wandering on a path, enjoying the scene. Clare did work on the land, but he tends to write poems about the work of others, while he is at leisure. He is not interested in his own work, but in observing how others complete the picture and work in tandem with nature. The action in the poem is partly natural and partly human, all blending together, the participles evenly spread between them.

'The Beans in Blossom' is very similar thematically to 'The Wheat Ripening'. Clare is wandering on a path, thinking, and enjoying the wind on his face, the scent of the beans in blossom, and listening to the blackbird's song. Rodney Lines, in his essay 'Clare's "rough country sonnets"'[3] calls this poem "a masterpiece", justifying his view with this appreciation:

> What Clare achieves in this sonnet above all is the freezing of time in a particular picture, while letting us know that nature is not static, for time moves as surely as the figure of the sauntering poet who takes us with him on his journey of delightful discovery. The dominant use of the letter 's' adds sound to the picture as well, so we can hear the breeze and smell the perfume of the beans.

Clare's summer poems can be compared to delicate watercolours of the landscape, with a strong sense of the particular light at the time. Yet there is so much more: the scents and sounds are captured too. 'The Beans in Blossom' is full of luxury: words like "luxuriantly" and "rich disorder" give this poem a sense of abundance, which is characteristic of summer. Clare admires the disorder in nature, as seen in the phrases: "wild music", "rich disorder", "toss the mole hills". It is full of sound, colour and scent, and presents a vivid sensuous experience of walking alone in the countryside. Clare's language engages the senses: "the southwest wind ... breathes"; and smell: "luscious comes the scent of blossomed beans", "clover blossoms ... Strong-scented". This sonnet has no people; it is populated with birds, cattle and insects. Only the poet is there, and he is not disturbing the scene. Clare's deictic[4] language:

I roam these new-ploughed fields and by the side
Of this old wood where happy birds abide

makes readers feel they are walking with him as he points things out. Clare often writes 'in the moment', which adds to the freshness of his verse. The sonnet's couplets offer a sense of joys accumulating as the poet walks and notices things. 'The Wheat Ripening' and 'Summer Tints' are written in more interlacing and gentle rhyme schemes, as is 'Summer Moods'. Clare's sonnets are innovative and do not always follow the Shakespearian or Petrarchan[5] models. He freely draws on the sonnet form to suit his own purposes.

'Summer Tints' is also a very accomplished poem. The personification of summer as an artist is a beautiful one, and Clare goes on with precision to describe the colours used by this artist: "Light tawny oat-lands", "lightly scorched green", "bleachy brown". The wind is "mixing the brown and green" as though the colours are being mixed on a palette, a stunning metaphor for the way the soft summer wind makes the crops ripple till the colours blend. The opening line tells us that this is high summer and nature's plenty is in full abundance: Clare is "bosom-deep in grain". The crops are just starting to ripen; there is no more than "tinges". The language is very evocative, as Clare points out "the checkered plain" and "nodding lands of wheat". Northamptonshire is fairly flat and it is possible to see for a long way. Clare's view here is certainly panoramic. He enjoys the sight of young people, "many a maid and clown"[6] making haycocks, a delightful addition to a summer scene. Haycocks now are rarely seen; instead hay is swathed in black plastic in the fields. Clare concludes by the observation that even busy shepherds have stopped work to admire the beauty of the scene.

Clare also wrote wonderful poems about autumn, but the Everyman selection does not include them. They are widely available in other editions of Clare's work.

NOTES

1 Chapter 2: 'He plods about his toils'.

2 Letter from John Taylor to John Clare, 4th March 1826, quoted in *Clare: The Critical Heritage*, edited by Mark Storey (Routledge, 1973).

3 *The Independent Spirit: John Clare and the Self-Taught Tradition*, edited by John Goodridge (The John Clare Society and The Margaret Grainger Trust, 1994).

4 Deictic language is 'pointing' language; it depends on context for its meaning, as though Clare is pointing at what he can see.

5 Shakespearian sonnets have a turn around line 12 and end on a rhyming couplet following quatrains in alternate rhyme. Petrarch's are organised into eight and six lines.

6 By 'clown' he means a young man who works on the land. He does not imply they are simpletons, as the word is sometimes used in Shakespeare plays, for example Perdita's adoptive brother in *The Winter's Tale.*

# 8

# The busy falling rain

Clare enjoyed rain and its effect on the landscape. Two of his rainy-day poems are included in this selection: 'The Summer Shower' and a sonnet, 'The maiden ran away'. The latter has been discussed in Chapter 2, where the focus was the countryside as a workplace. It has a comic tone, whereas 'The Summer Shower' is a more relaxed and reflective piece, though not without some humour of its own. Clare's stanza design here has two lines of iambic pentameter, undercut by two lines of iambic trimeter.[1] The rhyme scheme is alternate, which serves as a link between the different line lengths. This pleasingly varied form keeps the movement fresh in this sustained poem of 27 stanzas.

Clare begins the poem with a phrase typical of much of his nature poetry: "I love".[2] Clare takes pleasure in listening to the rain and its effects from the shelter of a canopy of leaves. "I love it well" suggests this is something that happens frequently. The shower is a welcome relief from summer's sticky heat, and the "pattering woods", a beautiful phrase that shows the wood as a place full of hidden life, shifts the focus from the sheltering poet to what he is sharing. All birds "trim" or groom their wings in the rain, but the genius of Clare is that we do not get blanket observations: he can distinguish one bird from another. The woodchat sings happily, the blackbird cleans "her sooty breast" while "squatting on her mortared nest". A lesser poet might have used the participle 'sitting' but Clare's word "squatting" is much more accurate. Like the poet, the blackbird is hidden from view in "the pathless wood". The pettichap too is observed by Clare as a sound, "nimbling", but because Clare spies the nest, he describes it in detail.[3] The pettichap is a summer visitor, migrating south in autumn, so Clare might particularly enjoy seeing its domed nest.

The shower grows heavier and Clare turns his attention to plants. He notes the effect of the leaves' shelter doubling the rain, as the water falls both from the sky and from the canopies. A striking metaphor records how beautiful the plants and rushes look:

> ... while the rain
> Strings their green suit with pearls,

The *s* alliteration and consonance, together with the long vowel sounds, make this image memorable and musical. The water drops appear cloudy, like pearls, because they reflect the cloudy sky. The plants are dressed in their best clothes and wearing jewellery.

Clare's imagination roams free as he imagines how people who were out in the rain are reacting, based on previous observations. A group of workers who were weeding between the crops take shelter under a large oak tree and pass the time by singing ballads and talking, but when they see that the rain will only get worse, they make a run for it and run laughing home. The metaphor "dimpling" to describe the stream is an apt one. Not only does it reinforce the happy laughter of the weeders, it is a precise observation on how the raindrops create indentations on the surface of the brook.

Clare's imaginings of the behaviour of this crowd changes the tone of the poem into a humorous one, as a girl slips and is embarrassed that her ankle, thought in those days to be inflaming of a man's lust, was on show, but half-glad to think that she has pretty ankles, until a young man makes an appreciative comment, when her modesty asserts itself and she will not climb the stile until an older woman tells him off and makes him behave. This thought would amuse Clare, as he too appreciated a pretty girl.

Another anecdote centres round a pack of boys out bird-nesting, a now illegal practice which involved stealing eggs from birds' nests. They are impeded on the journey home by an angry bull "with straining eye", as though nature itself disapproved of the activity. They have to go the long way round and arrive home bedraggled. By contrast, the ploughing team, even though dripping wet, is perfectly comfortable. The ploughboy is relaxed and singing as the horse splashes its way home, happy that the day's work is done. The horse contentedly 'Naps' the wet grass when it is released into the pasture. The gypsies too, remain unperturbed by the shower. The lark begins to sing in "smoking rain", another evocative metaphor which suggests the warmth of the summer's day as the water begins to evaporate, and mist rises.

The concluding six stanzas return to the relaxed tone of the start of the shower. People are now at home, unable to work any more that day. The land itself is refreshed. Even the planet itself is resting:

The cramped horizon now leans on the ground,
Quiet and cool, and labour's hard employ
Ceases while all around
Falls a refreshing joy.

Clare's stanza design allows for a dying fall here as the poem gently closes with the original idea of the low skies seeming to rest on the ground, worn out by the shower. The poem's structure has been deployed to document the shower from its first raindrops, through the height of the downpour, to its final cessation, which coincides with the ending of the day. Rain is necessary to the crops, and welcome.

NOTES

1 Five feet and three feet respectively, so that the third and fourth line are significantly shorter.

2 An example in the Everyman selection is 'I love to watch the evening crows go by', a sonnet in the 'Birds and Beasts' section.

3 Cf. 'The Pettichap's Nest' in the 'Birds and Beasts' section.

# 9

## Grasses that never knew a scythe

Although Clare loved landscape that was cultivated and wrote about the people who worked on the land, as he did himself, he had a special reverence for wild places where nature was allowed to go her own way. One such place was Emmonsales Heath, which was common grazing land, with areas of heather and gorse, as well as grassland. Villagers would use it as a source of fuel for cottage fires, their only means of heating. It was boggy fenland which must have nurtured many rare plants and birds before it was drained. Gypsy encampments would have been part of its attraction for Clare. Wild areas like this also provided a space for leisure and play. Some vestige of the heath remains in the nature reserve known as Castor Hanglands. The rest of it is now farmland. Clare wrote two poems about it, only one of which is in the Everyman selection.

Clare addresses Emmonsales Heath directly in this expansive lyric poem, personifying it. This would have seemed natural to him, perceiving the place as a friend, dressed in the "wild garb of other times", that is gorse or "furze", a thorny plant which clings to the land and bears golden blossom almost all year round, particularly in early spring. Words like "lazy" and "easy" show the relaxation the heath induces in Clare. The grasses are left free to "wave[s]", a friendly gesture, and the wild flowers blossom freely, never being cut down. The place is virginal because it has never been cultivated:

> Stern industry with stubborn pride
> And wants unsatisfied
> Still leaves untouched thy maiden soil
> In its unsullied pride.

The imagery here reveals Clare's attitude towards those who would destroy the wild places for their own ends, as rapists deflowering the untouched land. This is precisely what happened to many of Clare's sacred places during the infamous enclosures, but Emmonsales Heath did in part escape this pillage. Clare perceives it as a place of shelter for birds and animals from "savage men", and indeed some of the creatures Clare would have seen there have now disappeared from the area, such as the rare bird, the nightjar.

Many of the plants that grow there would not thrive on farmed land: "blooms that love what man neglects" indicates why the land has been left alone. Wildflowers are capable of thriving on very poor rocky land, or in boggy land on which crops would rot. Clare cites the scents of the wild rose and the woodbine. Wild roses bloom only once, unlike the garden varieties, and they produce rose hips, which are edible and particularly prized for their medicinal qualities. Young men like to wander on the heath and the young girls pick flowers to take home.

Clare introduces an important idea when he says:

> Creation's steps one's wandering meets
> Untouched by those of man;
> Things seem the same in such retreats
> As when the world began.

This stanza makes explicit the idea that the heath is an Eden, a garden of paradise from which humans were exiled by the disobedience of Adam and Eve in one of the creation stories from Genesis. The enclosures are represented in Clare's work by the notion of exile from Eden. When the wild places were fenced off and destroyed, original sin was committed that for ever ruined paradise for humans.

Clare's poem roams freely across the heath and points out its various treasures, much as a wanderer might find them. There is a brook to drink from and rest near: "One's weariness to soothe" and "spots amid thy bowers" where early spring flowers grow sheltered from the wind. It is a place where thoughts can stray freely, back to childhood days, and to feel at one with the birds and insects; even the ants, "pismires", in their anthill are happy. Clare says that anyone who does not secretly want to live there, or who does not appreciate it, has no "poesy". Paul Farley rightly links the heath with the lost content of childhood:

> … Clare's trees and heaths and quarries and bridges, together with the micro-climate of a Northamptonshire limestone heath, stand for the landscape of childhood we all end up leaving behind and looking back on … what we see… is somebody who has to keep returning to that first terrain.[1]

Clare refers to his boyhood walks and how he "stretched" them to include the heath where he could enjoy the solitude and be "nursed" by joy, when every living thing was singing from the pleasure of being alive. The kindness of the natural world struck him in those happy times:

> I thought how kind that mighty power
> Must in his splendour be
> Who spread around my boyish hour
> Such gleams of harmony.

This notion of seeing God in the landscape is called pantheism and is shared with several of the Romantic poets, notably Wordsworth[2] and Blake.[3] Clare was much more likely to go for walks on a Sunday than attend church, which he found dull. Seeing God around him in nature was far more pleasurable.

Clare's presentation of childhood has much in common with these poets too. Childhood is a time of freedom before adult ways have corrupted the spirit, as seen in Blake's *Songs of Innocence* and Wordsworth's *The Prelude*. The Romantic poets were followers of the philosophy of Rousseau, who believed in gently rearing children, educating them by allowing them to learn from experience (thus tempering natural instincts of self-preservation with absorption of social mores) and providing fresh air and exercise.[4]

Emmonsales Heath is also where Clare famously roamed too far afield and went "out of his knowledge" as he remarks in his autobiographical writings. The poem concludes with the idea of the sun creating a "halo" in "nature's wide and common sky", "common" here meaning belonging to everyone, and indicating Clare's attitude to the common land which was being gradually taken out of public ownership. The heath is one of his sacred places.

NOTES

1 Introduction to *John Clare Poems*, selected by Paul Farley (Faber and Faber, 2007).

2 For example, from 'Tintern Abbey':

> sense sublime
> Of something far more deeply interfused,
> Whose dwelling is the light of setting suns,
> And the round ocean and the living air,
> And the blue sky, and in the mind of man.

3 From *Auguries of Innocence*:

> To see a World in a Grain of Sand
> And Heaven in a Wild Flower,
> Infinity in the palm of your hand
> And Eternity in an hour.

4 *Emile* (1762).

# Birds and Beasts

# 10

# Is there no other bird

Clare's poems about birds are special because he does not only write about birds considered beautiful, such as the nightingale. He goes beyond convention and sees the beauty in crows and starlings and other common birds he observes around his home. Many of his bird poems are sonnets: this taut little form is perfectly suited to the taut machine of flight and birdsong that a bird is. In 'The Wren' he poses the question:

> Why is the cuckoo's melody preferred
> And nightingale's rich song so fondly praised
> In poets' rhymes? Is there no other bird
> Of nature's minstrelsy that oft hath raised
> One's heart to ecstasy and mirth as well?

The cuckoo is often used as a symbol: in this case of infidelity, from the birds' habit of laying an egg in the nests of other birds, leaving them to rear its young, for example in the Shakespeare song,

> When daisies pied and violets blue,
>     And lady-smocks all silver white,
> And cuckoo-buds of yellow hue
>     Do paint the meadows with delight,
> The cuckoo then on every tree
> Mocks married men for thus sings he
>                                         "Cuckoo".

Both cuckoos and nightingales are associated with spring, because they are migratory. Clare has a special fondness for birds which do not migrate but keep company all winter.

The nightingale is a potent symbol for so many of the Romantic poets. Keats has his 'Ode to the Nightingale', Wordsworth wrote 'The Nightingale', Samuel Taylor Coleridge includes his poem 'The Nightingale:

A Conversation Poem' in *Lyrical Ballads.*[1] Prior to the Romantics, Milton wrote a poem called 'O Nightingale', and Shakespeare associates the bird with lovers and refers to it in *Romeo and Juliet.* In Greek mythology, Philomela, a rape victim who has her tongue cut out, was turned into a nightingale. Homer and Sophocles write about nightingales. Clare must have encountered nightingale poems time and time again in his extensive reading, but very few about the birds he observes.

This is not to say that Clare does not value the nightingale. In his sonnet 'The Nightingale', he marvels at the "clod-brown" ordinariness of the bird that can so easily remain inconspicuous while making "thrilling music". Perhaps one of the reasons this bird's song is prized is that it sings only at a particular time of year, the time associated with love, springtime. It is often to be heard at night, though it does also sing in the daytime. Clare blends the description of dusk in spring with the hearing of the nightingale's song:

> This is the time when in the vale, grass-grown,
> The maiden hears at eve her lover's vows
> What time the blue mist round her patient cows
> Dim rises from the grass and half conceals
> Their dappled hides …

The lovers have stolen a moment for themselves while they are working, and the nightingale, as though prompted by their love, chooses that moment to sing. The ploughman on his way home is beguiled to stay and listen, and Clare comes up with a strongly visual line to illustrate the slow fall of dark, as the fields: "Lose all their paths in dusk to lead him wrong", as though the ploughman has been enchanted and is unable to leave the scene, held in place by the spell of the "sweet melodious song". In 'The Wren', however, Clare pleads the case for other birds having an equally delightful call, such as the wood robin. One only has to listen to recordings of birdsong available today on the internet to realise he is absolutely right. The wren is a loved companion who would often shelter and sing in the shepherds' hut where Clare was staying.[2] Ancient folklore holds the wren sacred and there are old customs associated with hunting the wren.

Clare also loves crows, stark black birds with a sinister reputation. The sonnet called 'The Crow' is devoted to them, whereas the sonnet 'I love to hear the evening crows go by' is an essay on the behaviour of birds in the evening, with the robin as the star of the show, occupying the last six lines. In the first of these sonnets, Clare shows us a crow flying, its dark plumage a strong silhouette against "the thin blue sky". He fondly calls them 'chimney-sweeps' because of their sooty feathers and recreates the sound of their flight in the beautiful onomatopoeic word "sosh" and the graceful "sail by", unperturbed by the March winds ripping into the trees. He makes no grand claims for their calls, or croaks, but enjoys them for what they are, an "exercise of croaking joy".

The second sonnet, 'I love to hear the evening crows go by' reads like a catalogue of some birds unnoticed by other poets but beloved of Clare: the crow, the starling ("starnel" in Clare's dialect), the sparrow and the pigeon are all closely observed and distinguished for us with wonderful economy. The sparrow is "bustling", then "plops" to rest on the house eaves, the pigeon "bounces", which is exactly how it moves, the starlings "darken down the sky" because they are large black birds with white spotted undersides. There is one general reference to migratory birds, called "stranger birds" because they are not natives. The behaviour of the robin is endearing because he does not fear humans and will come close "To watch the maiden sweeping out the crumbs". He is after those crumbs and will venture right up to people to take his prize, then find shelter in a farm building. His insouciance is a cause for joy to Clare. The phrase "I love", which starts this sonnet, is a favourite of Clare's, and can be found in many of his poems.

Clare also writes of less well-known birds. The 'Landrail'[3] fascinates him because its call can be heard but it is very difficult to see. The call flits from place to place with never a sight of the bird that makes it, so that it appears to Clare like "a fancy everywhere/A sort of living doubt". Everyone is trying to see the bird: the boys in their play and the shepherd's dog in its hunting, all to no avail, yet one will stumble over its nest when not really looking, once the bird has vacated it. Clare explains that it makes its nest in the dust, in a simple hole, in the wheat fields, when the crop is high and undisturbed. Another magical bird for Clare is the wagtail. The charming and much-anthologised poem 'Little Trotty Wagtail' is one of Clare's best-known poems, astonishingly written during his time in Northampton Asylum. It is a joyful, comic poem detailing the movements of the wagtail as he copes with a heavy rain shower. Words like "tittering, tottering", "waddled" and "waggle", "nimble" and "dimpling" all give a sense of fun and laughter, word play and inventiveness.

Clare's poem 'The Skylark' is about another bird beloved of poets. Many folk songs exist about the skylark too, associating it with the early morning when lovers must part and the ploughboy must go to work.

John Lucas notes that Clare is "an unrivalled observer and describer of flora and fauna".[4] Neither the hare nor the skylark "is a metaphor for the poet", unlike in Shelley's 'Ode to the Skylark'. In Clare's poem the hare, in the wonderful image "some brown clod the harrows failed to break", and the skylark are under threat from humans.

At the heart of this poem, there is a description of the skylark in flight, zigzagging across the verse form with Clare's flexible line breaks and swooping syntax:

> ... the skylark flies
> And o'er her half-formed nest with happy wings
> Winnows the air – till in the clouds she sings,
> Then hangs a dust spot in the sunny skies
> And drops and drops till in her nest she lies...

The lark can fly very high, so here it appears as a mere speck when in the sky, but can suddenly return to the nest in a dizzying descent. Both the hare and the nest are lying safely in the corn, but there is a sense that this haven may not be enough to protect them. Danger creeps into the poem, making the reader anxious for the creatures but knowing nothing can be done to protect them. Passing boys might imagine that if they were birds they would build their nest high, but the skylark builds on the ground. John Lucas sums this up nicely: "Delighted discovery, here as elsewhere in the bird poems of this period, is poised against a sense of threatening forces, always felt if not always seen."[5] Clare's bird poems are valued for their precise observations of birds, many of which are now endangered. He makes wonderful poetry from the strong visual and aural sense of wonder he creates in the reader.

NOTES

1 Published in 1798.

2 Shepherds would have to stay with their sheep for months at a time, when they were out to pasture, and a shack was often provided for them.

3 Also called a corncrake.

4 *John Clare*, Writers and their Work (Northcote House, 1994).

5 Ibid.

# 11

# Nature is the builder

As seen in 'The Skylark', Clare has a fondness for birds' nests. In the Everyman selection, 'Among the Orchard Weeds', 'The Nightingale's Nest', 'The Yellowhammer's Nest', and 'The Pettichap's Nest' all involve discoveries of birds' nests and detailed descriptions of them.

The sonnet, 'Among the Orchard Weeds', is different both in form and topic from the other three, because it is about a domestic bird. The others involve discoveries of wild birds' nests, whereas in this sonnet, Clare is delighted that the nest remains undiscovered despite the best efforts of the servant girl, whose job it is to find the eggs, and the Sunday boy, who hopes to discover some eggs he can take home. Both are bamboozled by the hen, which has cleverly protected her eggs by laying them "Among the orchard weeds". She plays a game of hide and seek with them: they can hear her "cackling" but cannot discover the nest, no matter how much trampling around is done. The happy outcome in the final couplet is that the chicks are brought "chirping to the door". The repetition of the hen cackling suggests that she is laughing at the humans because they are not only wasting their time but being stung by nettles.

The other three poems in the section are all invitations to come with Clare to find the nest of a particular bird, to observe it closely. This is most overt in 'The Nightingale's Nest', which begins:

> Up this green woodland ride let's softly rove
> And list the nightingale – she dwelleth here.
> Hush! let the wood gate softly clap – for fear
> The noise might drive her from her home of love;

The many soft vowel sounds here suggest music and warmth. Clare encourages his companion to be quiet, as the gate to the woods must only "softly clap", a suggestion of applause for the nightingale. The highly emotive phrase "home of love" shows Clare's empathy for the little bird, as home was of paramount importance to him. 'The Flitting' has a similar phrase: "I've left mine own old home of homes." No wonder he feels protective towards the nightingale.[1] The slightly archaic language is a nod towards the poetic nature of this bird.

Clare relies on his previous experiences of hearing nightingales, to guide the reader, his companion, to the correct site of the nest. It is by no means certain that he will find it; this poem is a quest. Clare recounts previous discoveries, after seeking for hours, crawling under 'matted thorns' and moss. The memories are sweet to him and he marvels that the bird could be so ordinary to look at while producing such a sublime song. He also invests the bird with human emotions:

> Her wings would tremble in her ecstasy
> And feathers stand on end as 'twere with joy
> And mouth wide open to release her heart
> Of its out-sobbing songs – the happiest part
> Of Summer's fame she shared …

Clare imagines that the bird is full of happy thoughts, but if there were the slightest sense of danger, she would fall silent, as though the only permitted audience were "the listening leaves". Even the thrush, hearing this song, would try to imitate it. Clare admires the thrush for trying but suggests that the nightingale, as a bird which migrates in winter, has fewer worries to "damp" his "ardour". This is expressed in a beautiful parallel phrase: "Her joys are evergreen; her world is wide." Clare's sympathy with the thrush is not surprising, given that he had a fondness for non-migrant birds, and that he was all too aware of the nightingale as a poetic symbol. He writes in a letter to Herbert Marsh in 1830, speaking of Keats:

> … as is the case of other inhabitants of great citys he often described nature as she … appeared to his fancys & not as he would have described her if he had witnessed the things he describes …

On the other hand, he disapproved of stuffed birds in glass cases. So in Clare's poems, he is at pains to be accurate and true to life, but not to be a natural historian. He enjoys, as he says in the letter, "to look on nature with a poetic feeling". Hugh Haughton puts this well in his essay 'Progress and Rhyme':[2] "Clare's position is a complex one, a balancing act." Clare's particularity is one of his strengths.

The rhyme scheme is loose and musical. This befits the theme of freedom and the musicality of the birdsong. Soft vowels predominate, which helps to create the quiet atmosphere that must be maintained if the bird's nest is to be glimpsed. When the bird is heard, Clare reminds the reader to be quiet:

> – Hark! There she is, as usual, let's be hush,
> For in this blackthorn clump if rightly guessed
> Her curious house is hidden – part aside
> These hazel branches in a gentle way
> And stoop right cautious 'neath the rustling boughs,

The sibilance of these lines imitates whispering, as Clare rummages around the undergrowth and shrubbery searching for the nest, careful not to disturb it in any way, or frighten the mother bird, but just to see it. In this section, he adopts the imperative mood. He is the expert and the reader is the novice being initiated into the secret knowledge.

The bird, sensing they are about to discover her secret, stops singing, but Clare turns his remarks to her, to reassure her that he means no harm:

> We will not plunder music of its dower
> Nor turn this spot of happiness to thrall,
> For melody seems hid in every flower

Clare's pathetic fallacy of all the surrounding plants appreciating the music, "bowing" and "blushing" is a magical way of detailing the woodland plants surrounding the nest: harebells, whose heads hang down, weighted by flowers, cuckoo pint (another name is Lords and Ladies) with its "spotted leaves". "Gaping" is an accurate and original way to describe its flower, which grows inside a green hood.

It is not until the final section of the poem that the nest is finally described in full. By this time, the suspense has been perfectly orchestrated, so that the reader is agog to see it. It is unique to the nightingale, and Clare describes it very precisely. His lexical choices suggest the poverty of the nest, an interesting contrast to the richness of her song, and a detail other poets, writing about this most poetic of birds, fail to mention:

> And little scraps of grass – and scant and spare
> Of what seems scarce materials, down and hair,
> For from man's haunts she seemeth nought to win.

Religious imagery enhances the notion of initiation. "Solitude's disciples" are the only humans likely to come near to the "hermit's mossy cell". Five eggs lie within the nest, like the bird, not at all beautiful "deadened green or rather olive brown", an indeterminate, sludgy colour. But within them is the "legacy of song" that the bird will leave to the woodland, should her nest remain undisturbed. Clare's poem is a powerful argument against the collecting of eggs for any purpose. Naturalists at the time would collect eggs to blow out the contents for their collections. Clare trusts his companion to refrain from such desecration.

The yellowhammer does not hide its nest as effectively as the nightingale. It takes Clare a few lines only to find it, following the clue given by the bird flying up in alarm at a boy scrambling down the bank. It is a simple nest, made amongst the river bank grasses, lined with horse hair. Clare develops a beautiful image from the fact that the eggs look as though they have been scribbled on, so the bird must be a poet. This is strong identification for Clare, who sees the bird as a fellow dweller in the world of imagination and rhyme. He likens the brook to Castaly, the fountain of the Muses who inspired poetry in Greek mythology. The nearby molehills, beloved of Clare as cushions to sit on when out walking, he connects to Mount Parnassus, where the Muses lived. Clare fears for the nest because it is known that sometimes snakes, such as adders, which live on river banks, will wait for the chicks to hatch and eat them as they leave the shell, leaving "a houseless home".

This conclusion is a re-enactment of the Fall, from the Book of Genesis, which tells us the story of the temptation of Eve by Lucifer taking the form of a snake. As a result of Eve's tasting the apple from the Tree of Knowledge, she and Adam are ejected from Eden. Clare's personal Eden is the time before the land enclosures, which left him to sing "mournful" just as these "little warblers" would if their chicks were lost. The theme of betrayal is subtle here, but suggested to Clare by his sense of the birds as poets. The poems about birds and birds' nests are very evocative, and, although they appear simple and accessible, when set into context with the rest of Clare's work, acquire a deep significance.

The three birds' nests poems in the Everyman selection are all in the present tense. The reader feels that the discoveries are made in real time and the suspense of the quest can be renewed on re-reading. Like the nightingale, the pettichap, or chiffchaff as it is more commonly known, is a migratory bird. 'The Pettichap's Nest' begins very informally, with a conversational "Well". Clare is chatting to the reader, expressing his surprise at the unlikely places this bird chooses to build. Although the nest is unprotected by plants and situated at the side of a well-used wagon road, it is so cleverly made as to be almost unnoticeable. As with the yellowhammer, what gives it away is that the startled bird had flown up as Clare and his companion passed. The nest is a curious design. The bird has taken hay from nearby stooks and combined them with oak leaves from the ditch to make an oven-shaped nest with a very small entrance hole. Inside, the nest is lined with down and feathers. There is something unmistakably erotic about these lines:

> Built like an oven with a little hole
> Hard to discover – that snug entrance wins,
> Scarcely admitting e'en two fingers in
> And lined with feathers small as silken stole
> And soft as seats of down for painless ease

Given that Clare was very familiar with the oral tradition[3] and its symbolism of the bird as the penis and the bird's nest the female genitalia, this sexual innuendo is natural and wholesome. Country folk were not given to prurience and Clare was admittedly "a lover very early in life".[4] Patty was expecting his child before they were married. For Clare, the sexual undertones indicate the tenderness of his approach to the nest and the care he takes with the "delicate" eggs, which are very small and "a faint and pinky red". The nest seems beleaguered with dangers detailed in five lines of anxiety; he calls it a "miracle" that they are as unharmed as if they were in the safest of places.

It is only at this point that the bird is revealed to the listener, when it returns to the nest. Clare expresses surprise: "Well I declare, it is the pettichaps." Its size is compared with the wren's, the smallest of birds. The observation takes the reader right back to the poem's opening. It is not the first time Clare has seen a chiffchaff's nest, but he has never seen one in such an open place before. Clare assumes the mantle of the expert in these poems, which is fitting, but it is a nice touch that even he is surprised here. This increases the immediacy of the poem.

John Lucas observes that all the poems about birds, and their nests, contrast the delight of discovery with the "sense of threatening forces"[5]. He goes on to say:

> … he is increasingly drawn to recognise the vulnerable frailty of the world of little things, as though his own predicament, isolation, sense of hurt, direct him to such frailty.

The birds' nest poems are significant in the context of Clare's work. Each nest could be compared to a poem, with its small weavings of twigs and organic materials. Each one is vulnerable to destruction, and each one attempts to increase the bird population in the face of loss of habitat because of the enclosures and other changes to the rural landscape at this time.

NOTES

1 See Chapter 15, where 'The Flitting' is discussed in detail.

2 In *John Clare in Context* (Cambridge University Press, 1994).

3 For example, the ballads 'The Cuckoo's Nest' and 'The Bird in the Bush', which are both very explicit in their treatment of seduction, use this symbolism.

4 Clare's *Autobiographical Writings* (Oxford University Press, 1983).

5 *John Clare,* Writers and their Work (Northcote House, 1994).

# 12

# The hedgehog hides

Animals also feature in Clare's poems. He prefers the small creatures which are often overlooked by other poets. This is partly because Clare empathised with them for their vulnerability and partly because he was able to observe such animals very closely. John Lucas contrasts his "empathy with a world of little things" with Wordsworth's "almost obsessive self-regard" in *The Prelude.*[1] Clare writes of the hedgehog, the mouse, ants and squirrels, in four sonnets in the Everyman selection. Beyond this selection, there are poems about the fox and the badger, both animals are preyed on by thoughtless humans. Moles are beloved by Clare, and he writes movingly of their deaths in his anti-enclosure poems, for example 'Remembrances'. Rabbits too, are hunted and trapped: Swordy Well is concerned for the rabbits that dwell there, in 'The Lament of Swordy Well'.

The hedgehog has a pair of sonnets, linked together by phrases in common, such as "muddy dyke" and words like "hunt" and "meat", appearing as two stanzas of the same poem. This double sonnet is a compendium of folklore about hedgehogs, combined with Clare's own acute observations. The animal has simple needs. It finds crab apples and sloes where they have fallen on the ground, near its nest under the hedge. Its ability to roll into a ball is a source of wonder, referred to twice in the poem. However, this self-defence technique cannot save it from the hunting dogs. The unobtrusiveness of the hedgehog, in words like "creep", and "hide", contrasts with the "noisy dogs" of the gypsies who want to catch the animal for food, even though its meat is "black and bitter". Others hunt the animal too, on the slender basis that it steals milk by sucking the cows' teats. Clare argues that this is not physically possible because its mouth is far too small. Clare's sympathies are strongly with the hedgehog, subtly shown without bombast, through lexical choices: "small head like a hog", "mouth scarce big enough to hold a straw" compared to the actions of its tormentors, who "hurl with savage force the stick and stone".

'One day when all the woods were bare' presents another beleaguered animal which is endangered today, the red squirrel. Clare does not reveal the owner of the nest until the final few lines. He piques the reader's interest when he spies "a strange-formed nest", at a time of year when birds are not nesting, because the woods "are bare and blea" (bleak). Clare's excitement is delightful:

> So up I scrambled in the highest glee
> And my heart jumped at everything that stirred.

The squirrel's movements are sudden and take him by surprise: "something bolted out ... a brown squirrel pattered up the tree". The discovery leaves Clare pondering on the amazing thing he has just seen. Both 'The Hedgehog' and this sonnet include incidental descriptions of birds seen at the same time. The former notes the magpie bathing in the dyke and the latter has a "startled pigeon buzzed from bouncing hawk". These additions suggest the richness of nature around Helpston and help the reader set each poem in context, as though Clare is helping the reader to focus binoculars to see one thing, against a background of many others.

'One day when all the woods were bare' and 'I found a ball of hay among the grass' continue the theme of nests from the poems about birds' nests, for birds are not the only creatures which build their own havens to raise their young. When Clare pokes (he uses the delightful dialect word "progged" which suggests he poked it with his foot) "a ball of grass", he accidentally discovers a mouse nest, where the mother is suckling her young. The sight is "so odd and so grotesque" that Clare comically runs away. He withdraws, hides and observes the mouse return to her nest. The poem concludes with a couplet describing the scene, with the sun glinting from the pools of water which are natural features of this area. "Cesspool" is water which collects on the land between a river and its bank.[2] This wide sweep of landscape in the final couplet swings the reader's vision away from the tight focus on the mouse's nest to the broad flat wetlands. This extraordinary visual technique emphasises the miniature size of the mouse babies and their mother, and thus their vulnerability.

Even smaller than the mouse is the ant, the subject of the final 'beast' poem. The sonnet is the perfect vehicle for the "ants' city", because it is a small tight house of iambic pentameters, small but cleverly made. This one has an intricate rhyme scheme of *ababbcbcddbebe*, which suits the intricacy of the ant civilisation as Clare perceives it:

Such government and order there to be;
Some looking on and urging some to toil.

He admires the way they help each other when a load is too large for one, even calling them 'fellow men'. He feels an affinity with the worker ants because of his own station in life, and thus devotes more lines to them than to the ones with different roles.

Clare expresses his sense of wonder in two magical images. In imagining "they speak a language whisperingly", he creates a feeling of secrecy which is intriguing and gives the ants human characteristics. The notion that they are the descendants of the fairies is charming, but Clare can back it up with his knowledge about them, in their "kings and laws", so it seems perfectly believable within the context of this poem. Clare lifts the lid of an ants' nest for us and uncovers all this magic and delight in an unpromising place like 'a woodland bank' or 'rotten tree'. This sense of wonder evoked by Clare returns the reader to a childhood state of grace, when every little thing is a cause of amazement. He slows time down and brings in the reader's focus sharply on these minute insects. Unlike the other poems discussed in this chapter, this poem is not about a specific ants' nest, but a reflection on the ant way of life in general.

The animals and birds people the landscape Clare celebrates and mourns in his poetry. The teeming lives supported by the land make it even more precious in his eyes. And because his vision is so precise and knowledgeable, he preserves both the land and the wildlife without causing harm, unlike naturalists who take eggs and practise taxidermy, or those who alter the land by enclosing it.

NOTES

1 *The Prelude*, published in 1850, is Wordsworth's autobiography of his soul, a prime example of the 'Egotistical Sublime'. Wordsworth writes of his feelings of guilt when he snared birds as a boy.

2 The modern meaning of 'cesspool', as a pit to collect sewage, did not come into use until the mid 19th century.

# Love

# 13

# Sweet the Pleasures

John Clare's poetry is characterised by love. "I love" is one of his most used phrases. His love of nature was profound. But he also loved pretty girls, seeing women as another of nature's gifts. He loved the feeling of falling in love and was very susceptible to the charms of women. Since the Everyman selection includes only eight love poems, giving just a flavour of one of Clare's most enduring themes, further love poems are quoted in full in the two chapters in this section.

Of the eight love poems in the Everyman selection, half are written in ballad form, like 'The Courtship', and could easily be sung, possibly to an existing tune. These are: 'Song: The morning mist is changing blue', 'First Love's Recollections' and the two titled as ballads. Clare was immersed in the ballad form from an early age: his father knew a great many of the folk ballads by heart. Many are narratives of lost love, as well as ghost and murder stories. The ballad stanza is written in iambic metre. The odd-numbered lines have four iambic feet and the even-numbered lines have three iambic feet. The shorter lines rhyme. Clare's ballads in this section also have the odd-numbered lines rhyming, resulting in an alternate rhyme scheme.

'Song: The morning mist is changing blue' recalls seeing a pretty girl go by on a beautiful spring morning. The "maid" "with inky hair" seems like another beautiful natural phenomenon, fitting the lovely morning, which is still early and fresh with the mist still present. One of the attractions of the girl is her smile and her happiness. Clare feels he is falling in love and experiences the pleasure of it together with the pain of knowing it cannot last. In the final stanza, the imagery links nature and the girl, through personifying nature "in her sweetest dress". Although this is a joyous poem, there is a bittersweet tone. Rhyming present participles deployed intermittently ('turning/mourning') give it a dying fall. It is a *carpe diem*[1] poem, about the transience of beauty.

'Song: Love lives beyond' is another philosophical poem about love. It has a complex stanza design, which has a dimeter (2 feet) followed by a tetrameter (4 feet), a second dimeter, and a trimeter (3 feet). This design with its varied line lengths creates a subtle, shifting music. The alternate rhyme scheme links together the different lines. The first stanza is repeated with some subtle changes at the end, like a refrain. Clare argues for the everlasting nature of love, and asserts his affection for "the fond, the faithful, young and true". He also tells us where he sees love – in nature, in spring and in young voices, drawing on the traditional association of lovers with the springtime. His imagery is synaesthetic;[2] for example he describes light and sunbeams as "music to the mind". This is a very gentle, soft and comforting poem in which Clare brings together many of the fleeting joys of nature, such as evening dew, sunbeams and spring.

'Love and Memory' also contemplates love and death. In it, Clare remembers a beautiful woman he knew, who has died. This poem is not about Mary Joyce,[3] who lived for another ten years after the poem was written. It is a moving hymn of mourning in which he imagines that the dead girl is happy now that she is in heaven, but that he is left to regret her passing and lament that he can see no one as beautiful. Similar imagery is deployed as in the other poems of lost love: flowers and blossoms dying, the circle of life mirrored in the seasons, day and night. It is accepting of death, seeing it as a natural part of life.

Another poem with a similar theme, but a different treatment of it is 'An Invite ['Invitation' in some editions] to Eternity'. This is one of Clare's asylum poems. It is a strange visionary piece in which he invites a "maiden" to join him in his quest for eternity. The reference to parents and sisters could be about his parents. His mother died the year he moved to Northborough, and his father died while he was in the asylum. He had a twin sister who died before reaching her first birthday. He felt isolated in the asylum, and this poem shows how he feels without nature to bring him pleasure. The scene he describes is apocalyptic. There are strong links with the poem 'I Am' in the final section of the Everyman selection. In both poems he longs for the peace death brings. The journey through to heaven is hazardous and risky, and the opening lines recall Psalm 23, 'The Lord is my shepherd'. Clare's "valley depths of shade,/Of night and dark obscurity" owe a clear debt to "Even though I walk through the valley of the shadow of death,/I will fear no evil,/for you are with me", with which Clare would have been very familiar. 'I Am' shows the poet to be lonely, so perhaps inviting a beautiful young girl to accompany him on the road to eternity was a comforting thought. The couplets of tetrameters are themselves comforting; the certain and sure full masculine rhymes sound confident and the whole poem is a series of questions hoping to draw an affirmative answer from his chosen guide.

The remaining poem in this section is a puzzling one until it is placed into context. 'Ballad: I dreamt not what it was to woo' tells how Clare was innocent of love till the robin instructed him. It is a rite-of-passage poem, or an allegory for the onset of sexual desire. Birds are often associated with love and sex, in ballad tradition and in poetry. If a robin pecks on a window, it means a child is about to be conceived. The robin is a symbol of compassion and fertility. It is also associated with love because of its red breast. George Deacon, in his book *John Clare and the Folk Tradition,*[4] demonstrates how Clare had been brought up in the tradition of folk song and would naturally use the same symbols: "It is little wonder therefore that sexual symbolism should appear in Clare's work; it would be more surprising if it did not." One such folk song has the lyrics:

Cock Robin got up early
At the break of day,
And went to Jenny's window
To sing a roundelay.
He sang Cock Robin's love
To pretty Jenny Wren,
And when he got unto the end,
Then he began again.

This song makes the bird symbolism very explicit. Clare is not the only Romantic poet to draw on this symbolism. In *Songs of Innocence*, William Blake writes this poem:

**The Blossom**

Merry, merry Sparrow!
Under leaves so green
A happy blossom
Sees you, swift as arrow,
Seek your cradle narrow,
Near my Bosom.
Pretty, pretty robin!
Under leaves so green
A happy blossom
Hears you sobbing, sobbing,

Pretty, pretty Robin,
Near my bosom.

Like Clare's poem, this is much easier to interpret when placed into the folk tradition. Poets tend to use these symbols in a much more subtle way than the often crudely obvious songs which were circulating at the time. But read this way, Clare's poem is a gentle exploration of the stirrings of sexual desire. The robin becomes a gentle guide, as though he is encouraging Clare to taste the joy of love at some point in the future:

He saw me to the town and then
He sighed but kissed me not,
And whispered "We shall meet again"
But didn't say for what.

The alternate rhyme scheme adds to the soft tone of wonderment, as the young man begins to realise the possibilities of love. The figure of Robin guides his footsteps and helps him over stiles as he walks him back to town. After this encounter, the young man can know no rest. Love is unsettling and potentially painful, yet we cannot do without it.

Clare's delight in the company of women, and the delicious feeling of being in love, is shown in this beautiful song from *The Midsummer Cushion*:

Sweet the pleasures I do find
Lovely Jessey near thee
When every green with flowers is lined
& linnets sing to cheer thee
Then my love so fair and kind
Tis heaven while I'm near thee – Jessey
Heaven while I'm near thee

Though tis not the charms of Spring
Can add a charm to cheer me
When every pleasure's took to wing
& left the pasture dreary
When every birds forgot to sing
Tis heaven to be near thee – Jessey
Heaven to be near thee
Left to winter's frost & snow

When storms descend severly
Left with birds to pick the slow[5]
And left with thee to cheer me
Still while life's red tide does flow
Tis heaven would be near thee – Jessey
Heaven would be near thee

Banished to some barren isle
Where famine scowled severely
Jessey blessed with thee the while
Till life was left to cheer me
Still on fate & thee I'd smile
Tis heaven to be near thee – Jessey
Heaven to be near thee

Who the Jessey addressed here is, is not known, but Clare's eye was taken by many pretty girls when he was single, and they often inspired poems. This song is interesting because it juxtaposes the love of nature with the company of a woman. In the first stanza, nature is blooming, birds are singing and the green is full of flowers. Clare finds himself in heaven, but stanza by stanza, each comfort is stripped away, until, moving through depression and wintertime, he still finds love a consolation even if he were banished from the nature he loves and was without even the most basic of comforts, such as food and drink.

Clare mentions many girls' names in his poems, but it is important to realise that poetry is not the same as biography. Bate cites only two serious relationships, though there were probably several flirtations. Betty Sell, a labourer's daughter, was one of them, but the other was Martha (known as Patty) Turner, whose family and friends did not really approve of him, but his better prospects remedied the situation, and her pregnancy by him encouraged them to see marriage in a different light. Clare married Patty Turner in 1820 and she was a loyal wife to him. Together they had a large family of children. He called her 'Patty of the Vale'. This extract from 'The Courtship' shows their first meeting:

Where are you going lovely maid
The morning fine & early
"I'm going to Walkerd", Sir she said
& made across the barley
I asked her name she blushed away

The question seemed to burn her
A neighbour came & passed the day
& called her Patty Turner

I wrote my better poems there
To beautys praise I owe it
The muses they get all the praise
But woman makes the poet

A womans is the dearest love
Theres nought on earth sincerer
The leisure upon beautys breast
Can any thing be dearer

I saw her love in beauty's face
I saw her in the rose
I saw her in the fairest flowers
In every weed that grows[6]

Clare draws on the conventional language of May Morning folk songs, in which a man meets a pretty girl and engages her in conversation, for example 'As I Roved Out' and 'Seventeen Come Sunday'. However, the poem soon lifts off into something original. The 'pretty maid' from convention becomes shy Patty Turner, to whom Clare pays a debt of gratitude. The description of their physical love as "leisure upon beautys breast" shows the importance of their physical relationship. The stability she gave him enabled him to write his best poems. Patty was also the one who sought some help for him when his mental health was failing. If Mary Joyce was the Eve in his Eden, Patty was his daily comfort.

NOTES

1 Seize the day.

2 Where one sense is described in terms of another.

3 Clare's relationship with Mary Joyce is considered in Chapter 14.

4 Published by Francis Boutle, 2002.

5 Sloe – a wild damson.

6 *Poems of John Clare's Madness*, edited by Geoffrey Grigson (Routledge, 1949).

# 14

# Where is the Heart?

For John Clare, no other pretty girl was enough to eclipse the memory of his first love, Mary Joyce, who was a classmate of his. He fell in love with her because of her pretty face and quiet personality.

This beautiful poem, not included in the Everyman selection, shows the profound effect she had upon the impressionable and sensitive boy:

**First Love**

I ne'er was struck before that hour
With love so sudden and so sweet,
Her face it bloomed like a sweet flower
And stole my heart away complete.
My face turned pale as deadly pale.
My legs refused to walk away,
And when she looked, what could I ail?
My life and all seemed turned to clay.

And then my blood rushed to my face
And took my eyesight quite away,
The trees and bushes round the place
Seemed midnight at noonday.
I could not see a single thing,
Words from my eyes did start —
They spoke as chords do from the string,
And blood burnt round my heart.

Are flowers the winter's choice?
Is love's bed always snow?
She seemed to hear my silent voice,
Not love's appeals to know.
I never saw so sweet a face

As that I stood before.
My heart has left its dwelling-place
And can return no more

The gentle alternating rhymes express harmony and music as he contemplates the quiet dignity of the girl. Clare expresses the well-known symptoms of falling in love in a fresh way. It is telling that imagery of nature and of music is deployed, and the wintry imagery expresses the hopelessness of his love, though he silently imagines she feels the same: "she seemed to hear my silent voice". Clare contrasts heat with cold and day with night. The poem expresses a defining moment for him; love has changed him for ever without a word being exchanged. Although they were attending the same school, she was the daughter of a well-to-do farmer and thus out of his reach, or so he imagined.

We do not fully know how well he knew Mary Joyce: he writes as though he had a relationship with her, but in *John Clare: By Himself* he admits: "She was a beautiful girl and as the dream never awoke into reality her beauty was always fresh in my memory."[1] However, he never forgot her and she became as a muse to him.

Mary Joyce was a symbol of lost love, lost opportunities and lost youth for Clare. Nicholas Birns suggests that Clare finds consolation for the loss of Mary in nature: "The loss that is mourned is that of Mary, and nature provides a consolation."[2] This idea can be borne out in two of the poems discussed here: 'First Love's Recollections' and 'The Spring returns, the pewit screams'. Jonathan Bate astutely comments:

> On the one hand, he is a youthful Don Juan, filling up a book with the names of girls who have taken his fancy before he has even grown any hair on his face. On the other hand, his platonic love for Mary Joyce, which begins and ends in his own imagination, constitutes the whole course of his amorous career. He remained obsessed with the idea – the ideal – of love as something unobtainable. The greater the distance from his classroom crush on Mary, the more it took on the aura of the one great passion of his life. Being associated with the years before puberty, the passion for Mary was kept free from the taint of sexual desire.[3]

But as Bate points out, Clare's love for Mary is innocent. Because of the link to childhood, the dream of Mary is his dream of childhood and freedom to roam. Mary is linked to the remembrance of the unspoiled Eden of his youth. As Mark Storey explains:

> The image of Eden was a natural one: but for Clare it was … much more than a simple literary trope … Just as he had lost the Helpston he knew, so he had lost his girlfriend, Mary Joyce. This was the meaning of his Eden: in it he had caught a glimpse of the innocence of love and nature, the real love for which he hankered for the rest of his life, ideal because it never blossomed.[4]

'First Love's Recollections' is a reflection on lost love and specifically names Mary. It recalls lovers' meetings and partings. There is some beautiful imagery here, much of it nature imagery: for example he likens the lost love to a bud than could not grow to flower:

> A fate like this has oft befell
> E'en loftier hopes than ours;
> Spring bids full many buds to swell
> That ne'er can grow to flowers.

This image shows Clare accepting the fact that his first love was never to grow to blossom. The poem began with the idea of rosebuds keeping their 'fragrance till they die', just as first love stays with the lovers for ever. The memory of his love for Mary sustains him, even though the poem is built on contrasts, as each happy reminiscence is balanced out by the present absence of her from his life. Typical of Clare, it is a poem full of loss and regret, but also the pleasure of the past and the fleeting nature of happiness.

However, sweet and sorrowful as 'First Love's Recollections' is, it explicitly describes a physical relationship ("how rapturous to thy lips I clung") which is not biographical. It is Clare's fantasy. When he was ill and in the mental asylum, he imagined that he was married to Mary as well as to his actual wife, Patty. In a letter he wrote from High Beech Asylum, he compares his love for Mary Joyce with his love for Patty:

> My dear wife Mary, I might have said my first wife first love and first everything – but I shall never forget my second wife and second love, for I loved her once as dearly as yourself and almost do now so I am determined to keep you both for ever.[5]

This letter shows his mindset of Mary as his spiritual wife and Patty as his earthly one. Mark Storey sees the dichotomy as being the way Clare views Mary as the symbol of things lost, like the countryside surrounding Helpston before the enclosures, whereas Patty is his wife of the unsatisfactory present. Storey's perception about the impulse behind Clare's work helps to clarify these confused emotions:

> Much of his poetry is a retrospective act of piety, a searching into the corners of memory, an attempt to create out of his losses a permanence denied him in the present.[6]

As an example of this 'retrospective act of pietry', 'My Early Home' is a hymn to his childhood home, and the country surrounding it, where he rambled freely as a boy. Clare views the land before the enclosures as an Eden, combined with his youth, his awakening as a poet and his innocent love for Mary Joyce.

**My Early Home**

Here sparrows build upon the trees,
    And stock-dove hides her nest:
The leaves are winnowed by the breeze
    Into a calmer rest;
The black-cap's song was very sweet;
    That used the rose to kiss;
It made the paradise complete:
    My early home was this.

The redbreast from the sweetbrier bush
    Dropt down to pick the worm;
On the horse-chestnut sang the thrush,
    O'er the house where I was born.
The moonlight, like a shower of pearls,
    Fell o'er this 'bower of bliss',
And on the bench sat boys and girls;
    My early home was this.

The old house stooped just like a cave,
    Thatched o'er with mosses green;
Winter around the walls would rave,
    But all was calm within;
The trees are here all green again,
    Here bees the flowers still kiss,
But flowers and trees seemed sweeter then;
    My early home was this.

Clare's memory of his childhood home is dominated by birds: sparrows, doves, blackcaps, robins and thrushes are all part of the soundtrack of this poem. Characteristically, Clare gives the reader a busy scene, full of active verbs, yet to the ordinary passer-by, nothing would seem to be happening. But the language of love is subtly threaded into this poem. Doves and roses are common symbols for love, and the verb 'to kiss' occurs several times. The poem recalls carefree days where the old house was an emotional as well as physical shelter from both actual storms and storms of the mind. The imagery is characteristically original, for instance, "the moonlight, like a shower of pearls" suggests the rain as well as the luminescent glow of the moon, and the consonance of "light" and "like" makes soft music in the reader's ear, which combines with the birdsong to create harmonies. The crux of the poem is in the last few lines, in the notion that everything in the past 'seemed sweeter', even though birds still sing and trees still make leaf. Although Mary Joyce is not mentioned in the poem, nor indeed is any woman, her presence in Clare's past innocent days suffuses the whole poem.

Another poem from the Everyman selection which expresses the loss of Mary Joyce is 'Ballad: The Spring returns, the pewit screams', in which Clare recalls or constructs a precious time spent with Mary, when he gave her a daisy, a flower associated with purity, innocence, loyal love, beauty, patience and simplicity, a very apt choice. Unlike the previous year, the spring brings him no pleasure, because he has lost her for ever. The pewit seems to be making a harsh sound, whereas last year its cry was 'music'. It is rooted in a particular place: "by this bridge", which gives it a sense of immediacy, as we listen to Clare meditating on what he has lost, in a place which has happy associations. The happy memory contrasts throughout with the sorrowful present, and it seems to him that they might as well be parted by seas, as the few miles between them. Mary Joyce never married, but the reference to her 'leaning to wealthy praise' may refer to Clare's assumption that her father had aspirations for her.

'Song: Say what is love?' attempts a definition of love, but concludes with the thought that though he may not know what love is, he does know its whereabouts:

> Say what is love? – whate'er it be,
> It centres Mary still with thee.

The poem is written in rhyming couplets, in tetrameters.[7] It uses a question-and-answer structure, and Clare uses caesura to separate the question from the answer. This gives the poem a halting, hesitant mood, as does the use of binary oppositions, such as prison versus freedom, and life versus death, which express Clare's ambivalent attitude to love, also portrayed in 'Song: The morning mist is changing blue'. Love is both sorrowful and joyful. It is fleeting but everlasting, "a rose leaf on the page of fame".

John Clare's poems to Mary Joyce are among the most poignant of his works. His poems about the enclosures are full of righteous anger as well as mourning and loss. Clare does sometimes show anger towards his lost love, blaming her for the fact that circumstances kept them apart. It is difficult to separate his fantasies about her from the facts, but in his head she broke his heart, as shown in this 'Song', written after his return home to Northborough from High Beech:

**Song**

Heres were Mary loved to be
And here are flowers she planted
Here are books she loved to see
And here the kiss she granted

Here on the wall with smiling brow
Her picture used to cheer me
Both walls and room are naked now
No Marys nigh to hear me

The church spire still attracts my eye
And leaves me broken-hearted
Though grief hath worn their channels dry
I sigh o'er days departed

The churchyard where she used to play
My feet could wander hourly
My school walks there was everyday
Where she made winter flowery

But where is angel Mary now
Loves secrets none disclose 'em
Her rosey cheeks and broken vow
Live in my aching bosom.[8]

This song is a lament for Mary, her absence haunting familiar objects and places. The poem begins in his home, more likely to be Helpston than the Northborough cottage Mary would never have visited, but it moves from there to Glinton, where Mary lived, its spire a constant reminder of her as it dominated the landscape. This spire makes him recall the churchyard where they would walk and play in schooldays, but poignantly the final stanza rests in her unknown whereabouts, and the lack of fidelity which he imagines came between them. The rhyme scheme is entirely composed of soft vowel rhymes which produce a tone of sorrowful lamentation. Mary Joyce died in a house fire at the age of 41. By the time he was writing this 'Song', and the love letter written at High Beech, she was already dead, having never married. Clare refused to believe the facts and persisted in his notion that he was married to her as well as to Patty, and had children with both women.

Two poems in which Clare continues to express his love for Mary and his missing her from his life, are not included in the Everyman selected poems, but are well worth examining.

In 'It is the Evening Hour' Clare explores a visitation by Mary's spirit. It is a consolatory poem built on contrasts. According to Storey, "Clare rises above any commonplaces of nostalgia or sentiment, without in any way straining the lyric form he has chosen":

It is the evening hour,
  How silent all doth lie:
The hornéd moon he shows his face
  In the river with the sky.
Just by the path on which we pass,
The flaggy lake lies still as glass.

Spirit of her I love,
  Whispering to me,

Stories of sweet visions, as I rove,
  Here stop and crop with me
Sweet flowers that in the still hour grew
We'll take them home, nor shake off the bright dew.

Mary, or sweet spirit of thee,
  As the bright sun shines tomorrow,
Thy dark eyes these flowers shall see,
  Gathered by me in sorrow,
In the still hour when my mind was free
To walk alone – yet wish I walk'd with thee.

The first stanza sets the scene and creates an atmosphere suitable for a gentle haunting, with the quiet, the calm lake and the river reflecting the crescent moon. Storey rightly points out Clare's choice of pronoun as the plural first person, 'we'. Mary is already with him as the poem begins, as though we are observing a lovers' tryst. His wishes to see her have summoned her up and she speaks to him, although she is not there. The contrasts are carefully balanced to express his joy at thinking of her and his sorrow that she cannot be physically present. Her 'dark eyes' contrast with 'the bright sun' which he will see tomorrow, yet he will not shake the dew from the flowers, as that would be to dismiss his fantasy of being with her. Similarly, he is both alone, yet accompanied by Mary. As Storey puts it, "it is a poem of opposites which do not cancel each other out." Impossible things are true because Clare wishes it so, just as perhaps he imagines himself married at the same time to both Mary and Patty.

The ballad, 'Where is the Heart' is a farewell to Mary, where he accepts he will never see her again. This poem was included in *The Rural Muse* (1835) and expresses perfectly how love's ideal has deserted him. He feels he can never love anyone else as purely as he did Mary. There is a sense of inevitability in this poem which is not present in all of the Mary Joyce poems. Rhetorical questions explore the impossibility of forgetting her:

**Ballad: Where is the Heart?**

Where is the heart thou once hast won
Can cease to care about thee
Where is the eye thou'st smiled upon
Can look for joy without thee
Lorn is the lot one heart hath met

That's lost to thy caressing
Cold is the hope that loves thee yet
Now thou art past possessing
Fare thee well

We met we loved we've met the last
The farewell word is spoken
O Mary canst thou feel the past
& keep thy heart unbroken
To think how warm we loved & how
Those hopes should blossom never
To think how we are parted now
& parted, oh! for ever
Fare thee well

Thou wert the first my heart to win
Thou art the last to wear it
& though another claims akin
Thou must be one to share it
Oh, had we known when hopes were sweet
That hopes would once be thwarted
That we should part no more to meet
How sadly we had parted
Fare thee well

The song is imbued with a sense of what might have been. Its tender and accepting tone is full of regret. Never again can such love be hoped for; his heart is permanently damaged by their parting. Words like "lorn" and "cold" contrast with the warmth of their love and the sense of promise he felt, suggested in the line "those hopes should blossom never", where the stress falls on the last word, partly through its placing and partly through the opposite rhyme word "ever". The gentle rhyme scheme, with the dying fall created by the polysyllabic rhymes "caressing/possessing", "spoken/broken" and "wear it/share it" contributes to the sorrowful tone. The dominance of open vowel sounds makes this song perfectly suited to being sung.

Clare is not generally thought of as a love poet. However, this is a mistake which arises from a desire to categorise poets. Clare has been long thought of as a nature poet and indeed, he does excel in this; however, it is part of his greatness as a poet that he can shine in other areas. Had Clare written no nature poems, his love poems would be sufficient to earn him the label of love poet, though there is far more to his work than any one aspect of it. His skill and craft as a poet are summed up by Mark Storey, when he says, "It is part of Clare's achievement that he is able, in so many poems, to maintain a fluidity of line that works in harmony with the formal pressures he applies." This is as true of his love poems as of the rest of his oeuvre.

NOTES

1 *John Clare by Himself* (Carcanet, 2002).

2 In his essay '"The Riddle Nature could not Prove": Hidden Landscapes in Clare's Poetry', in *John Clare in Context* (Cambridge University Press, 1994).

3 *John Clare, A Biography*, by Jonathan Bate (Picador, 2003).

4 *The Poetry of John Clare*, by Mark Storey (Macmillan, 1974).

5 *Selected Letters of John Clare*, edited by Mark Storey (Clarendon Press, 1988).

6 Mark Storey, *The Poetry of John Clare.*

7 Lines of four iambic feet.

8 From Byron, *Childe Harold.* The punctuation is as in Clare's original.

# Loss and the Politics of Nature

## 15

# I thought them all eternal

'Remembrances' is a heartbreaking poem. It looks back fondly on the kind of childhood joys described in 'Sport in the Meadows'. Now that summer is over, the games the children played in the fields appear to Clare like "visions". These pleasant carefree times stand for the summer of life. This notion is made more explicit later in the poem when Clare says the enclosures were "a Winter" because the fields were "sudden bare". Clare recalls many of the games he himself used to play, and his pastimes, such as trying to catch fish with "crooked pins and thread" and making swings on tree branches. However, undercutting these joyful memories, the sense of loss is present in every stanza. He and his family had moved three miles from Helpston to a larger cottage,[1] which took him away from these familiar places, which in any case had been despoiled by the enclosures. Clare is also mourning the fact that he is no longer a carefree boy; he yearns for a return to those innocent times. Children lack the sense of the preciousness of their childhood days, unlike adults looking back.

As well as being full of a sense of loss, 'Remembrances' is also bitter in its reflections on the enclosures. Clare compares them to the arch-enemy of the time, Napoleon Bonaparte:[2]

> Enclosure like a Bonaparte let not a thing remain,
> It levelled every bush and tree and levelled every hill
> And hung the moles for traitors – though the brook is running still.

This picture of the countryside, of moles hanging from trees, killed because they were seen as pests, and left to swing in the wind as a warning to others, and of natural features being destroyed, is dark and uncomfortable. Clare does not soften the horrors; he feels them keenly. Clare's reference to the moles, using the beautiful dialect word "mouldiwarps", also stands as a metaphor for the protesters in the Swing riots, who were hanged for their part in the destruction of threshing machinery in 1830.[3] This political comment may have been a reason that this poem was rejected from *The Rural Muse* by Clare's editors, Mr and Mrs Emerson. For John Lucas,[4] this metaphor is key:

> The hung-up bodies of the moles, to which Clare returns more than once, become an iconic image of loss, of wilful destruction, of brutal power. It is as though his imagination fixes with almost obsessive concern on those helpless unfortunates who are endlessly victimised by new laws and who, in losing their small space of earth, can the more readily be destroyed. For now they belong nowhere, can claim no identification with place. 'Remembrances' is about loss of place: 'place' may stay vividly in the mind but in all other senses it is simply disappearing or has already disappeared.

The evils of enclosure are man-made. They go beyond the ordinary hardships brought on by winter, cold and hard work. Land which had been under common ownership was fenced off and made out of bounds. The 'owners' showed no respect for natural features; turning the land to profitable use was their objective. This horror is made all the more potent by the way Clare names particular places he loved, like Sneap Green and Puddocks Nook, which he has seen destroyed by humans. Further examples of the way the land sustained people can be seen in this poem, such as "haws[5] like sugar plums" and "bramble[6] bushes". Clare foregrounds the beauty of the plants which grew there, such as "the daisies gemmed in dew", to accentuate the loss of such precious beauty. He also refers to particular trees, such as "Lea Close Oak" and "old Round Oak". "Swordy Well" commands its own poem: it was one of Clare's sacred places.

The poem's form serves the sense of mourning: the short last line allows a dying fall. John Lucas[7] points out how the shift in metrics underscores the change of mood in each stanza: "the sudden shift from anapaest[8] to the heavy insistent stresses of iambic". The move to iambic increases the stresses, creating a sadder, heavier line.

Contrast is at the heart of this poem. Clare constantly compares the past with the present, saying his heart was "just like a feather – now as heavy as a stone". "Langley Bush" still goes by its name, but the bush has been uprooted. The commons are "levelled like a desert by the never-weary plough". Clare's imagery is forceful:

> And boyhood's pleasing haunts like a blossom in the blast
> Was shrivelled to a withered weed and trampled down and done,

The fragility of the "blossom" is contrasted with the force of the "blast", emphasised by the alliteration of the 'b' sounds which link the opposites. Further alliteration in the "withered weed" and the harsh "down and done" strengthens the impact of the lexical choices. "Shrivelled" and "withered" chime vowel sounds creating a musical effect swallowed up by the phrase "trampled down and done", with its harsh finality and firm consonants.

The poem ends with a personification of joy as a beautiful young woman whom Clare should have wooed and begged to stay. For lack of this, she has "left the paths of men". He says that "love never heeded to treasure up the May", as though joy was queen of the May (hawthorn blossom) and humans did not appreciate her or worship her as they should. Paul Chririco points out the pun Clare makes on poesy and posey, in his essay 'Writing misreading: Clare and the real world':[9]

> We are clearly pointed to the etymological connection between 'poesy' and posey: "& gave her heart my poesys all cropt in a sunny hour" ... This is a generic transformation of the specific memories encountered earlier in the poem into the conjectural relations of allegorical figures of love, beauty, joy and the lonely poet.

Clare has a gift for blending such literary constructs with real places and things. It is an astonishing achievement that he makes the reader see not only the loveliness of these very particular scenes and memories, but realise their significance and universality. This poem speaks to everyone, in a voice that moves effortlessly down the centuries. Robert Lynd's[10] comment that Clare "is more like a twentieth-century poet than an eighteenth-century poet" is prophetic, as Clare has commanded much more critical appreciation in more recent times than ever he received in his lifetime. Lynd compares Clare's work favourably with what he calls "the sonorous generalisations of Thomson's *Seasons*". Clare looked up to Thomson, who was one of his early influences,[11] but he eventually transcends him. Few now read Thomson with pleasure, whereas Clare's followers continue to grow.

'Remembrances' is a deeply felt and very moving poem. Clare's intimacy with the surrounding landscape is remarkable and it is expressed with outstanding compositional skill.

## NOTES

1. Lord Milton gave him the use of a cottage in Northborough in 1832.
2. Napoleon I (1769–1821), became emperor in 1804. His armies conquered much of Europe.
3. Nine of the rioters were hanged and 450 sentenced to be transported, despite the fact that no one was hurt during the riots. Property was damaged, a crime which was always severely punished.
4. 'Clare's Politics', Lucas' essay in *John Clare in Context*, edited by Haughton, Philips and Summerfield (Cambridge University Press, 1994).
5. The fruit of the hawthorn, valued for food.
6. Blackberries were useful for making wine as well as suitable as a dessert or pie filling.
7. *John Clare*, Writers and their Work (Northcote House, 1994).
8. Anapaests are often used in light verse. They begin with two unstressed syllables before the stressed one comes.
9. In *The Independent Spirit: John Clare and the Self-Taught Tradition*, edited by John Goodridge (John Clare Society, 1994).
10. Writing in 1921. This is from an unsigned review and quoted in *Clare: The Critical Heritage*, edited by Mark Storey (Routledge 1973).
11. Clare attributes starting to write poetry to reading Thomson's *The Seasons* for the first time.

# 16

## Every tree is strange to me

Clare's move to Northborough in 1832 occasioned the writing of 'The Flitting', one of the most evocative poems about home imaginable. John Lucas believes it is "one of the great poems of the nineteenth century".[1] The poem begins mournfully:

> I've left mine own old home of homes,
> Green fields and every pleasant place;
> The Summer like a stranger comes;
> I pause and hardly know her face.

The music of these lines is brought about through the long soft open vowels in the first line, particularly in the O sounds of sorrow, then the sibilance that follows in line two, the alternate rhymes and the regular metrics of the stanza design. Clare's perception of the summer as a stranger is because he has not experienced summer in Northborough before. It is not the same as summer in Helpston. The new cottage was three miles away from his native village, but the landscape was very different. He devotes the second stanza to the heath, and uses the poem to walk on it again in memory. The little details that he loves are typical of Clare:

> I miss the heath, its yellow furze,
> Molehills and rabbit tracks that lead
> Through besom ling and teazle burrs
> That spread a wilderness indeed;

It is not the animals themselves Clare is drawing our attention to here, but the evidence left by them. Their freedom to exist in peace is worth more to him than sighting them. Ling is heather, which could be used to make brooms, or besoms. Teazle is a tall biennial plant. Its flower-heads, which are full of stiff burrs, are used to raise the nap of woollen fabrics.

Furze is another name for gorse. These are common moorland plants, extremely tough, which make the heathland difficult to access. They provide the perfect cover for birds and animals.

Clare's opening lines to several of the stanzas show him in a range of positions: sitting in his "corner chair" and walking down the lane. He is restless. His mind goes wandering to all the places he loves but cannot now reach: "Heaths, woods and pastures, sunny streams". He remembers the trees he used to lean against, the molehills covered with moss he used as seats. His title for the collection in which this poem appeared was *The Midsummer Cushion*, after a custom of cutting a square of turf to bring indoors, to enjoy its summer flowers, like an indoor garden. These lines are a reference to his title, which was changed to *The Rural Muse* by the Emersons,[2] his editors:

> Where moss did into cushions spring
> Forming a seat of velvet hue,
> A small unnoticed trifling thing
> To all but heaven's hailing dew.

Clare's inability to settle in his new home is contrasted with the relaxation he felt among the familiar sights of his "home of homes".

Another thread Clare develops is the idea that birds sound different in Northborough. Clare had an intimate knowledge of birdsong and might well have been able to discern a variation. In praise of his old home, he asserts that even the crow, with its harsh cawing, "Croaks music". He remembers sitting on his "old bench" hearing the "sailing" buzzard's "shrill 'peelew'", which seems sweeter to him than the birds he can hear in Northborough. He can still hear the nightingale, but it sounds homesick, like him.

The poem expands in topic as Clare seeks solace. He relives his cherished memories of home and turns to reading for comfort. However, he is disappointed because fashions have changed; he prefers the older styles. This could be a reference to the fact that none of his later books enjoyed the same success as the first, *Poems Descriptive of Rural Life and Scenery*. The section from the ninth stanza onwards powerfully recalls this speech from Shakespeare's *As You Like It*:[3]

> Now, my co-mates and brothers in exile,
> Hath not old custom made this life more sweet
> Than that of painted pomp? Are not these woods

More free from peril than the envious court?
Here feel we but the penalty of Adam,
The seasons' difference; as, the icy fang
And churlish chiding of the winter's wind,
Which, when it bites and blows upon my body,
Even till I shrink with cold, I smile and say
"This is no flattery: these are counsellors
That feelingly persuade me what I am."
Sweet are the uses of adversity,
Which like the toad, ugly and venomous,
Wears yet a precious jewel in his head;
And this our life exempt from public haunt,
Finds tongues in trees, books in the running brooks,
Sermons in stones, and good in every thing.
I would not change it.

The Duke is contrasting life at court with the simpler life in the forest. Clare was familiar with Shakespeare from his own reading, and here is fully in sympathy with the view expressed by the Duke. For Clare, the "pomps of chivalry" are entertaining but not real, only shadows.[4] For truly sublime things, one must turn to nature. He compares himself to David, when he wrote the psalm 'The Lord is my shepherd'. King David himself was a shepherd before he killed the giant Goliath, and the well-known Psalm 23 speaks of the comfort of pastures and quiet streams. Clare points out that pomp passes away just as Shelley does in his 'Ozymandias' sonnet. David's poetry remains, but will be outlasted in its turn by "the little moss".

In a stanza which powerfully recalls the familiar words of the psalm, Clare speaks of the scenes in Northborough as "mere shadows" compared to his native village where he was happy:

By quiet woods and gravel springs
Where little pebbles wear as smooth
As hermits' beads by gentle floods,
Whose noises doth my spirits soothe

The simile about the pebbles is highly tactile and illustrates Clare's ability to find God in nature. His memories of making swings in trees sheltering from the rain in a hollow trunk, climbing trees to find birds' eggs, and other joyful times, comfort him now, where "every tree is strange to me".

For Clare, trees are individuals.

He refers to his lost fame when he says about nature, "she's a fame that never tires". Clare was fêted in London and met several of the literary figures of the day, with the publication of his first collection, but fashions changed and the literati lost interest in him. He had been introduced as a "peasant poet", something of a novelty act. But the novelty wore off and his poems about the enclosures could not be construed as pretty nature poems, although they represent some of his best work. They were too 'political', too critical of his 'betters' and too uncomfortable.

Clare speaks of how nature kept him company, how molehills used to "talk" to him, how sheep would praise summer, and "every weed and blossom" would welcome him. These plants and animals grew in Eden and deserve as much respect as humans. Lambtoe is the local name for bird's-foot trefoil, a tiny plant whose yellow three-pronged flower has delicate red veins. This, and the "May-bloom with its little threads", whose white flowers have tiny white stalks sticking up from the centre resembling little cotton threads, will outlive anything humans can create. Clare's magical simile, "like fairy pins", is not only accurate but beautifully conveys the sense of wonder he feels. He includes further Bible references to emphasise their historicity.

The twentieth stanza takes us back once more to the Shakespeare speech. Clare rejects London and all its glamour and false airs "where muses play on golden strings", using the word "shame" about their grandeur and falsity. Clare's own muse, on the other hand, "Bears wreaths of native poesy". The two stanzas that follow give a full description of the joys of this muse and the things she points out to him, such as "A hermit moorhen's sedgy nest". These thoughts lead Clare back to compare his new home with his old one. He must, as a gardener, destroy the weed shepherd's purse,[5] because it will kill the plants he needs to grow to feed his family. However, he finds it painful to do so, because it reminds him of his old home, where it also grew. Douglas Chambers, in his essay 'A Love for Every Simple Weed: Clare, Botany and the Poetic Language of Lost Eden',[6] calls the reference to shepherd's purse "a classic example of his technique of making the significant from the apparently insignificant". He goes on to make a larger claim:

> Clare ... historicises and enculturates this weed as a text, not only of himself but of a lost society. In doing so he creates a mythology of permanence in which his own isolation becomes part of a larger historical myth.

The poem closes with a reflection on how all things must pass, and nature will prevail. Writing the poem seems to have comforted him to some extent. He accepts he has had to say goodbye to the "Ivy at the parlour's end,/The woodbine at the garden gate". These are friends to him:

> But times will change and friends must part
> And nature still can make amends.
> Their memory lingers round the heart
> Like life, whose essence is its friends.

Like many a bereaved person (and losing his home was a bereavement to him) Clare realises that no one can take away his memories. A 'flitting' is a dialect word for moving home, but it also reflects the way Clare's thoughts flit about in the poem. As he meditates on what he has lost, his thoughts fly from Helpston to Northborough, to London and to the future when "still the grass eternal springs/Where castles stood and grandeur died".

NOTES

1 In *John Clare*, Writers and their Work (Northcote House, 1994).

2 The Emersons were friends. They meant well but were misguided.

3 Act II, Scene 1.

4 Actors were often called 'shadows' in Shakespeare's time, as in Puck's speech which closes *A Midsummer Night's Dream,* "If we shadows have offended/Think but this and all is mended."

5 Sometimes called Farmer's Ruin.

6 In *John Clare in Context* (Cambridge University Press, 1991).

# 17

# I'm Swordy Well

Swordy Well is one of Clare's sacred places. It is situated south of Helpston on the way to Peterborough. Because it was a field that had been quarried for stones since Roman times, it was hollowed out and was thus a safe haven for the wild animals and birds Clare loved. It was also a place where gypsies could camp, a fact which is included in the poem as a source of pride. Stone from Swordy Well was used for great cathedrals such as Ely and Peterborough. The name comes from a legend that an ancient sword was found by its spring. The place is known more recently as Swaddywell, the words having been corrupted over time. Since the poem was written, it has been used as a bomb dump, a landfill site and a race track, but was restored to a nature reserve in 2003.[1] Bate calls it a "modest Utopia",[2] which gives an idea of its beauty and importance.

It is likely to be Swordy Well that Clare refers to in his poem about rain, 'The maiden ran away'. He concludes that sonnet with the lines:

> E'en the old stone pit deep as house is high
> Was brimming o'er and floated o'er the top.

By the terms of the Enclosures Act of 1809, Swordy Well was granted to the overseers of the roads in the parish and ceased to be independent land. This meant that many wild things could no longer find a home there, and that the land would be used for profit, to its detriment. Clare's sonnet, 'The Passing Traveller' recounts the sense of awe a walker might experience to see "a deep and ancient stone pit full of trees", which again could be Swordy Well. The source of the "wonder" in the poem is that the depth of the pit allows humans to see nature from a different angle, from above:

> The passing stranger oft with wonder stops
> And thinks he e'en could walk upon their tops
> And often stoops to see the busy crow
> And stands above and sees the eggs below.

Clare repeats the word "wonder" twice in the poem as a noun, and once as a verb. He also repeats phrases for emphasis: "deep" occurs three times in the first two lines, qualified by "very" in the third time. He contrasts the squirrel who "dances up and runs across" the trees, while the humans can only stare. The place is a keeper of secrets too, so deep it could hide a church.

'The Lament of Swordy Well' gives the land a male voice, and we see its fears that it will cease to exist except in name. The voice of Swordy Well speaks for all who have been forced onto the parish's charity. Many humans are in the same case: exploited and then abandoned; for example, John Clare's father, Parker Clare, ended up breaking stones to earn a pittance, after a lifetime of working the fields. He suffered from rheumatism, but there was no financial help to enable him to retire. The very people who suffered most from the land enclosures were the ones who had to carry out the labour of fencing off and stripping the land, a cruel irony.

The voice is strong and powerful, sustained by the apt choice of the ballad stanza.[3] The sense of pride and independence is present from the start, when it criticises those who seek favours. By contrast, the personality of Swordy Well is one that will not beg nor solicit sympathy. Instead there is anger:

> I'm Swordy Well, a piece of land
> That's fell[4] upon the town,
> Who worked me till I couldn't stand
> And crush me now I'm down.

Clare expresses his own anger through the outspoken voice he has created. The land speaks out against bondage and ownership, its loss of independence and its poverty in the face of profit to be made. This is exactly how the lower classes felt: they too were losing their independence and freedom, exchanging these prizes for enslavement and increased poverty.

The land has been stripped and no nourishment put back:

> I've got among such grubbing gear
> And such a hungry pack,
> If I brought harvests twice a year
> They'd bring me nothing back.

The seventh stanza refers to the Napoleonic War, which, combined with a run of bad harvests, caused the price of corn to rise. This allowed profiteers to exploit the hungry. Here the very land itself feels similarly exploited.

The voice of the land is strongly colloquial. Clare's ability to imitate real speech is very modern. The double negative for emphasis was a feature of Middle English. Clare includes it in the idiolect of Swordy Well:

> … I never pin
> No troubles to my breast …

Clare also captures the inversions of speech in the fifth line of this beautiful stanza:

> The silver springs, grown naked dykes,
> Scarce own a bunch of rushes;
> When grain got high the tasteless tykes
> Grubbed up trees, banks and bushes,
> And me, they turned me inside out
> For sand and grit and stones
> And turned my own green hills about
> And picked my very bones.

The natural speech idioms make the voice of the land sound true and earthy. This stanza shows how the land has been raped. The rushes, compared to clothing, have been culled from the springs, which now are "naked": no plants adorn the banks or provide nesting grounds for water birds. The three lists are lengthened by the repeated conjunctive "And", to show that greed has no bounds. The verb "grubbed up" is a masterly choice, making the exploiters sound like grubs, lower life forms who are grubby in their pursuit of money, small-minded and indifferent to beauty. In the next stanza, he calls them "things" who were "born but yesterday". They have no sense of the past, or what the land has done, such as "built the town below". Mining the land is compared to the workhouse for people. At the time, there was no relief for old or infirm people. People who were unable to keep themselves, or had no family to house them in their dotage, they were sent to the workhouse, where the genders were separated. They worked for their bed and board till they died as paupers.

In the eleventh stanza, there is a topic shift to the fate of the wildlife after the enclosures. The bees cannot find any blossom to feed on, and therefore die, worn out with their search. Words like "feeble" and "almost-weary wings" pull at our heartstrings. The rabbits leave "my poor abode" as the land can no longer provide a home. They too "dread a workhouse". If a flower appears it is immediately cut down. The butterflies cannot stay without food. Because the stones have been removed, there are no sheltered places where a beetle can hide. Even the single tree has been cut down and "left a stump", which sounds ugly.

Clare draws a poignant contrast with the past:

> In Summers gone I bloomed in pride;
> Folk came from miles to prize
> My flowers that bloomed nowhere beside
> And scarce believed their eyes.

Now even the grass is being ripped away and the land has "scarce a rag to wear", like a beggar whose clothes are tattered, whereas once they were richly made. Now people no longer come to visit this parcel of land because there is nothing left to see. The land feels lonely, despite being "full of clack" to the reader; the sorrow of Clare's presentation of Swordy Well is that there is no one else to listen, except an unknown reader of the poem. People do not stop to listen any more and even the birds do not stay. Clare had times in his life where he felt lonely, such as when he moved to Northborough, and in his time in the asylums of High Beech and Northampton, so his notion of the loneliness of Swordy Well, whose only visitors now are those who come to raid its treasures, rings true. The land no longer knows its own face.

'The Lament of Swordy Well' was unpublished in Clare's lifetime: the subject was uncomfortable because it makes a political statement of protest, yet it is one of his finest ballads.

NOTES

1 The Langdyke Countryside Trust established Swaddywell Pit nature reserve in 2003.

2 *The Song of the Earth* by Jonathan Bate (Picador, 2000).

3 Ballad stanza: that is alternating lines of iambic tetrameter and iambic trimeter (4 feet/3 feet) with an alternate rhyme scheme.

4 Meaning 'nearby'.

# 18

# Unbounded freedom

The enclosures changed the face of the English countryside for ever. Old pathways were blocked off, trees were cut down, land was parcelled into small, hedged and fenced fields, so the openness of the landscape was lost, along with the open-field system of farming and the sense of community that accompanied it. The old way of life was lost also, as many customs vanished for ever. In the sonnet 'I dreaded walking where there was no path' (in the 'Country Year' section), 'The Moors' and 'The Fallen Elm' all articulate the effects of the enclosures.

'I dreaded walking where there was no path' is written in couplets, which expresses the sensation of being restricted. Clare feels trapped and "cautious", because he is trespassing. The first two couplets express his dread of being caught, but the call of the land is too strong, as we see in the first turning point:

> Yet everything about where I had gone
> Appeared so beautiful I ventured on …

His guilt follows him even when he has returned to the road "where all are free". He considers "How beautiful if such a place were mine", feeling he could care for the land better than its owner, but his poverty means he will never be in that position. Clare cannot feel "at home" on someone else's property, so that the pleasure he feels in nature is tainted by remorse. The enclosures created more and more pieces of land like this, with signs up saying trespassers would be prosecuted. Clare ridicules these signs in 'The Moors':

> A board sticks up to notice "no road here"
> And on the tree with ivy overhung
> The hated sign by vulgar taste is hung
> As though the very birds should learn to know
> When they go there they must no further go.

The verb "notice" is unexpected, as though the very board itself is surprised by what is written upon it. Negative words like "hated" and "vulgar" are apt. Clare demonstrates the pettiness of humans: as if they could prevent birds from flying where they wish! Nature cannot be bounded by man and birds cannot read such signs.

'The Moors' is one of Clare's most bitter poems about the enclosures. He begins by expressing a sense of awe in the sheer beauty and expanse of the moors, which have endured for "centuries" of "Unbounded freedom". Clare's language is carefully chosen to show the scope of the land:

> Still meeting plains that stretched them far away
> In unchecked shadows of green, brown and grey.
> Unbounded freedom ruled the wandering scene
> Nor fence of ownership crept in between.

Clare emphasises the unspoilt vastness of this land, whose only boundary is the sky. "Unchecked" is a stunning visual metaphor, because when land is carved up into fields, its appearance is chequered with the different crops. "Checked" also means 'stopped', an apt word for what enclosure has done to the ancient beauties of the common land. The line: "Though centuries wreathed Spring's blossoms on its brow" at once reminds the reader of the ancient Greek custom of crowning its heroes with wreaths, linking to the past, but also reinforces how worthy of celebration the land is. Using the negative prefix 'un' in "unchecked" and "unbounded" captures the contrast between then and now at the start of the poem. The word "prospect" was often used about picturesque views that were created by the landscape gardeners of the period, such as Capability Brown.[1] What Clare is pointing out here is that the moors were picturesque in reality, art done by nature's hand, not human, and therefore far greater than pale imitations could hope to achieve. No garden, however large, could fully achieve the landscape of the great moor:

> One mighty flat undwarfed by bush and tree
> Spread its faint shadow of immensity
> And lost itself, which seemed to eke its bounds,
> In the blue mist the horizon's edge surrounds.

The unbroken stretch of moorland described so exquisitely here is divided into "little parcels little minds to please", destroying its expansiveness and interrupting the mighty view, which was previously only curtailed by a natural boundary, the horizon, a boundary it transcends. Clare repeats the word "little" to brilliant effect in this poem. In lines 47-9, he uses it three times in succession to mean the petty minds of those enclosing the land, and the small fields it is now divided into. In lines 51–3 he uses it to engage our protectiveness towards "each little path" and the "little flowers" which cannot defend themselves against the mighty destroyer. In line 67, he returns to the word, once again using it for small-mindedness:

> Each little tyrant with his little sign
> Shows, where man claims, earth glows no more divine.

The divinity of the landscape is reinforced by the vastness of the moors. In addition to pantheism, Clare also powerfully suggests that the land before enclosure was a kind of Eden, and now it is destroyed; man can no longer walk there in joy and peace.

The bulk of the poem, after the word "now" in line 15, is devoted to detailing the different ways enclosures have ruined the moors. Clare's contrasts are beautifully drawn, for example the parallel phrasing in these lines:

> Free as Spring clouds and wild as Summer flowers
> Is faded all – a hope that blossomed free
> And hath been once no more shall ever be.

The language of prayer is reversed here showing enclosure is a sacrilegious act. The ancient prayer, 'Glory Be to the Father'[2] includes the line: "As it was in the beginning, is now, and ever shall be, world without end. Amen." The resonance of prayer serves Clare's tone as well as strengthening his argument.

Clare preferred to go for walks rather than to church on Sundays. He admits in his autobiographical fragments:

> I got a bad name among the weekly church-goers forsaking the "church going bell" and seeking the religion of the fields tho I did it for no dislike of church for I felt uncomfortable very often but my heart burnt over the pleasant pleasures of solitude and the restless revels of rhyme …

For Clare, then, the enclosures were tantamount to the destruction of the monasteries and the sacking of churches during Tudor times. If anyone doubted that Clare was a political poet, they only have to read these lines:

> Enclosure came and trampled on the grave
> Of labour's rights and left the poor a slave;

Clare is outspoken in his criticism. John Goodridge and Kelsey Thornton, in their essay 'John Clare: The Trespasser',[3] call 'The Moors' "a classic of protest literature, and a great poem". They rightly praise its "impassioned rhetoric, its mixture of righteous anger and elegiac sadness, its dramatic contrasts of time and and space". John Lucas agrees: "Its confident use of the language of popular radicalism is immeasurably helped by the hammering rhetorical rhymes which punch the argument home."[4] The poem's central section details how animals are affected by the enclosures. In the past, both cows and sheep found their freedom there when they were put out to pasture. Now the plover can no longer fly free, nor can the lark. Boys can no longer collect and eat mulberries as the bushes are all uprooted, and flowers no longer flourish there. The briar is the wild rose. It is unclear whether people collected the flowers to plant in their gardens, or the rosehips to make into syrup, but either way people are poorer from the lack. Clare's imagery gives a sense of the loss:

> ... sky-bound moors in mangled garbs are left
> Like mighty giants of their limbs bereft.

This is a horrific simile of a butchered giant tortured and left for dead. The cowslips and daisies which covered the ground are gone, likewise the poppies, or "headache". The flowers chosen here represent different seasons, and allow the reader to see the changing colours which clothed the giant, now that these fabrics of gold, white and red are left in tatters, 'mangled'. Another meaning of the word "mangled" is a process that happened to clothes after washing: they were passed through two rollers to squeeze out the moisture. Both meanings are apt for what has been done to the flowers.

Clare emphasises the damage done, and evokes our sympathy, in the pathetic fallacy[5] of the penultimate couplet:

And birds and trees and flowers without a name
All sighed when lawless law's enclosure came;

The paradox of "lawless law" is full of bitterness arising from the inability to prevent what the law is endorsing, even when it is morally wrong. The final couplet expresses this impotence:

And dreams of plunder in such rebel schemes
Have found too truly that they were but dreams.

From the vastness of the moors to one particular tree, the destruction caused by the enclosures was heartbreaking. Lee Close Oak, a large and ancient tree, was cut down. Clare noted in his autobiographical fragments that the carpenter who bought it "hearing it was a favourite tree of mine made me two rules".[6] 'The Fallen Elm'[7] is a lament for a tree which grew in the garden at Clare's cottage in Helpston. Bate[8] calls this poem "one of his starkest attacks on the hypocrisy whereby 'improvement' and enclosure are embarked upon in the name of 'freedom' but bring only oppression". The much-loved tree becomes a symbol for the irreparable damage that was done to nature at this time.

The first part of the poem sets up the tree as a close friend and neighbour: "Old Elm that murmured in our chimney top". The tree grows next to the house and can be heard by those inside. It shelters the cottage from the worst of the weather: "We felt thy kind protection like a friend." The pronoun 'thy' shows how warmly Clare felt towards the tree, since this form was used when addressing close friends and family.[9] He compares the tree to domestic things, such as the wind "rocked thee like a cradle to thye root", which emphasises the kinship of the tree to humans. This imagery strengthens the idea that chopping down the tree is tantamount to murder.

The beauty and the value of the elm change with the seasons. Clare's language is highly visual and original in his descriptions, and this poem is no exception. The winter storms:

... when dark tempests mimic thunder made
While darkness came as it would strangle light
With the black tempest of a Winter night

are contrasted with the 'sweetest anthem' of autumn. The tree's endurance is praised, for being able to keep its leaves green even when summer brought little rain and the earth at its base was 'iron'. Children played under the tree and the thrush, locally called a 'mavis', made his nest there. Clare even sees the tree as a poet:

> Thou owned a language by which hearts are stirred
> Deeper than by a feeling clothed in words;
> And speakest now what's known of every tongue,
> Language of pity and the force of wrong;

In the first section of the poem, there is a semantic field of language "murmured", "anthem", "whispering", "upbraid", which prepares the reader for the notion of the tree as a poet and singer. Later in the poem, Clare calls it "music-making". By contrast, it can have a more strident voice:

> Thou'st heard the knave, abusing those in power,
> Bawl freedom loud and then oppress the free.

This is the voice of the person who is responsible for the felling of the tree, in the name of freedom. Clare wrote this poem in a fit of outrage. In the event, the owner of the land changed his mind and the tree and its companion were saved. However, many other trees were disposed of.

The attack on the treatment of the poor is very strong:

> Though comfort's cottage soon was thrust aside
> And workhouse prisons raised upon the site.

In other words, the comforts of the poor were destroyed without thought and nothing put in place to help them, just workhouses, akin to prisons, to punish them for the 'crime' of poverty. Clare deplores the topsy-turvydom of people thinking they can own nature and do as they will with it, by law: "to wrong another by the name of right" and because "wrong was right and right was wrong".

If people can chop down a tree, reasons Clare, they can also destroy greater things, such as the moors: "The common heath, became the spoilers' prey." This highly charged political poem, like many of his other protest poems, was not published in Clare's lifetime. John Lucas admires its "rhetorical grandeur, the dramatic force of its public utterance" which "seems to me unequalled in English poetry".[10] The poem has its sweetness in the description of the tree; its bitterness is in the greed and ingratitude of those who would destroy something far greater than themselves for monetary gain. It is the same theme as Milton's *Paradise Lost.* It is impossible to deny, when reading Clare's poems about the enclosures, that he is one of the great poets. As Timothy Brownlow puts it: "It is the sadness and anger of a whole people that Clare articulates."[11] Whether writing of the heath, or a single tree, Clare sings of the lost England, the forgotten Eden of our wild places, and gives them immortality.

NOTES

1 Lancelot Brown (1716–February 1783), nicknamed Capability Brown, was a landscape gardener for many of the great houses of the period. 'Picturesque', meaning 'like a painted landscape' was all the rage in the mid 18th century. Vistas of gently undulating lawns, trees, lakes and streams were artificially created to mimic nature. The irony is that enclosures were destroying natural landscapes at the same time as the gentry was desiring them.

2 Lesser doxology, 'Gloria Patri'.

3 *John Clare in Context* (Cambridge University Press, 1994).

4 *John Clare,* Writers and their Work (Northcote House, 1994).

5 Attributing human feelings to non-human things.

6 Rulers.

7 The poem is usually titled 'To a Fallen Elm'.

8 *John Clare: A Biography* (Picador, 2003).

9 As in the French 'tu', where you is equivalent to 'vous'. The distinction has been lost from English, though is extant in 'Our Father… hallowed be *thy* name'.

10 *John Clare,* Writers and their Work (Northcote House, 1994).

11 *John Clare and a Picturesque Landscape* (Clarendon Press, 1983).

# John Clare, Poet

# 19

# Into the living sea of waking dreams

In 1837, Clare was admitted to Matthew Allen's Asylum at High Beech in Epping Forest. He had suffered what today would be termed a nervous breakdown. The move to Northborough, the death of his mother in 1835, the early deaths of some of his children, poor sales of his book *The Shepherd's Calendar,* financial anxiety and a tireless devotion to writing when he often went sleepless and unnourished, brought about a failing of both physical and mental health. Signs of his malady had appeared some years earlier and he had been treated by Dr Darling in London. Matthew Allen's Asylum was a private one, and Clare was cared for kindly, allowed to go for walks, read and write whenever he pleased. His physical health certainly improved.

'Sighing for Retirement' welcomes living in the asylum and Clare writes of the simple pleasures of peace, quiet and nature. The ballad stanza suits the gentle sentiments of relaxation through nature. The line: "The book I love is everywhere" restates the argument from 'The Flitting', also seen in other poems of Clare's such as 'Decay, a Ballad', that nature is herself the greatest book of all. It is a book anyone can read, that can be found anywhere. He pays homage to the "book" which gave him all his poems:

> I found the poems in the fields,
> And only wrote them down.

This comment may seem disingenuous, but Clare is looking back at his life's work and realising how important nature has been as an inspiration. He has tried faithfully to record what he has observed in a way that allows his readers to share the experience. He often wrote outdoors. In the context of the poem, these lines make him the recorder in words of the treasures in the great book of the fields. He is not being an apologist, but being true to this extended metaphor which recurs throughout his work. In this poem he welcomes the withdrawal from his daily cares:

And quiet Epping pleases well,
    Where Nature's love delays;
I joy to see the quiet place,
    And wait for better days.

After two years in the asylum in Epping Forest, Clare, terribly homesick, left on foot and walked the 80 miles home, sleeping rough and living on grass and plants, supplemented by the occasional handout. It took him four days. When he returned home, he was still mentally ill and suffering from delusions. He was convinced he was married to his childhood sweetheart Mary Joyce, who had died while he was in the asylum, as well as his actual wife Patty. He was only home for a few months before he had to be admitted to the asylum in Northampton, where he was to remain until he died in 1864. He was still writing poetry. Convinced he was Byron, whose funeral he had seen in London, he rewrote some of Byron's poems. At other times, he thought he was a famous boxer.

Despite his mental problems, he produced some of his most accomplished poems during the asylum years. 'I Am' is arguably Clare's most famous poem. It is certainly one of his most anthologised. It captures many of the themes of his work and is written without a trace of self-pity, even though he looks back on his life as a "shipwreck". In the first stanza, he admits he is lonely and has no one to talk to about his troubles. The line "I am the self-consumer of my woes" is reminiscent of the traditional idea of a 'sin-eater'. This is a folk magic practice which happened in rural areas, in which the sins of the dead person were symbolically consumed in the form of bread, by a volunteer, who also uttered a blessing over the corpse. Clare's metaphor here is that he has to eat his own sorrows, as no one is willing to take them away from him. He does this with some degree of success, because they "rise and vanish". He is amazed at his inner strength: "And yet I am, and live."

The first two stanzas are run on over a masterly stanza break. The pauses Clare builds in, are a crucial part of the music of the poem. The first stanza ends with the line: "And yet I am, and live – like vapours tossed", and the second stanza continues that thought, which is itself broken off from the rest of the first stanza by the caesura after "live". The reader has to be plunged into a long pause before we know where the "vapours" are going:

Into the nothingness of scorn and noise, –
    Into the living sea of waking dreams,
Where there is neither sense of life or joys,
    But the vast shipwreck of my life's esteems;

The stanza break gives the reader a taste of that 'nothingness', before Clare picks up the argument and returns to fluidity. The movement of the poem so far is like the rise and fall of a huge storm wave, preparing the reader for the shipwreck image. Clare has ridden high in his life, was praised and celebrated when his first book was published, only to be plunged down again when subsequent work failed to achieve the same success, even though he was developing as a poet. All his hopes of earning a living through his work came to nothing. He was doing all this for his loved ones, yet now they are "stranger than the rest". It was not easy for his family to travel the twenty miles to visit him in the asylum, and some of his children died before he did. Mary Joyce was lost to him but he did not believe that she was dead.

The last stanza is self-contained and brings the poem to a beautiful conclusion. Clare is longing for prelapsarian times, a return to Eden, a place without human beings, where there is just himself and God, where he can rest "as I in childhood, sweetly slept". The final couplet is full of peace:

Untroubling, and untroubled where I lie,
The grass below, above the vaulted sky.

The penultimate line expresses in neat antithesis his desire for freedom from all his worries: "untroubling" because he does not want to continue to cause anxiety for his family and friends, and "untroubled" because worldly cares such as fame and money made life unbearable. The last line is the perfect expression of peace, in calming antithesis: "the grass below" him as though he is lying on his back looking at "the vaulted sky". The metaphor "vaulted" is redolent of cathedral ceilings. To Clare, the outdoors was his church and the sky his church roof. This poem is often read as a wish for death, but what Clare really wants is to start again in a world without people, even women, and live a life of pure innocence, in the Garden of Eden, to be an Adam without Eve, without the Fall: an impossible dream, and all the more poignant because he knows that. John Lucas agrees with this assessment:

> He isn't wishing himself into his grave. Instead he yearns with a hopeless intensity for a pre-lapsarian, unfallen, unenclosed world, free from both the allure and sufferings of women and the threatening tread of men.[1]

'A Vision' repeats this theme of longing for peace, but in a far less apocalyptic way. Written in iambic quatrains, the poem works through contrasts to record a retrospective view of Clare's life:

> I loved, but woman fell away;
> I hid me, from her faded fame:
> I snatched the sun's eternal ray, –
> And wrote 'till earth was but a name.

In this comforting dream, Clare knows his poetry will be read in future years, that his work will make his name "immortal". All his life's disappointments are negated by this hope, and he rejoices in the fact that he kept his spirit 'free', that he did not give in to those who wanted him to change his style, however well-meaning they were.

A more detailed treatment of the ship-in-a-storm image from 'I Am' occurs in the ballad 'A seaboy on the giddy mast'. The first stanza sets up the metaphor. From the heights of the mast, giddy because the ship is being tossed by waves, the midshipman can only see the storm and hear the wind. Clare compares his own situation to the seaboy's. From his current vantage point, all he can see is the storm:

> My life hath been the ocean storm,
> A black and troubled sea.

But it has not always been thus. The third stanza remembers happier times, the "Bright gleams the morning gave", only to be destroyed by the storm. The sea is a strong metaphor for inconstancy, the fickleness of public taste Clare suffered from, and in this poem, he longs for a safe harbour or a calm sea. "every hope appears a grave" because at any moment the ship of his life could be swallowed by the storm, engulfed in its "wild inconstant blast". The word "raves" has overtones of madness: the mental problems Clare suffered must have been terrifying and always threatening to swallow his identity. His madness was the "tempest of his life", and he was acutely aware of his own difficulties. He told a visitor to the asylum in 1860, the writer Agnes Strickland: "They have cut off my head and picked out all the letters of the alphabet – all the vowels and consonants – and brought them out though the ears; and then they want me to write poetry."[2]

Clare lived life very intensely. Nature and love transported him to ecstasy. Ecstasy is akin to madness. Clare's poetry and his mental difficulties are intertwined to the extent that Clare was said by his doctors to be insane after 'years addicted to poetical prosings'.[3]

NOTES

1 *John Clare*, Writers and their Work (Northcote House, 1994).

2 Quoted by Roy Porter in his essay 'All Madness for Writing', in *John Clare in Context* (Cambridge University Press, 1994).

3 Quoted by Jonathan Bate in his 2003 biography (Picador).

# 20

# In poesy's spells

In 'Decay, a Ballad', 'The Eternity of Nature' and 'Shadows of Taste', Clare explores ideas about the nature of his subject matter and his theories about creativity and taste. 'Decay, a Ballad', from the section 'Loss and the Politics of Nature', laments the loss of poetry from his life. He remembers being able to write poetry but now he cannot do it: his muse has left him. The opening line, "O poesy is on the wane" appears as a refrain as the penultimate line in every stanza. He reflects back on past memories, recalling scenes he loved in the first six stanzas. He preferred wild land to any garden:

> The bank with brambles overspread
> And little molehills round about it
> Was more to me than laurel shades
> With paths and gravel finely clouted …

Douglas Chambers takes these lines as an indicator of Clare's writerly aesthetic. Clare enjoyed Keats' work (they shared a publisher) but criticised his tendency to refer to Greek mythology:

> The frequency of such classical accompaniment makes it wearisome to the reader where behind every bush he looks for Venus & under every laurel a thrumming Appollo. In spite of this his descriptions of scenery are often very fine … [1]

According to Chambers, Clare is stating in 'Decay' that the poetry of artifice is not the "true poesy", just as gardens are artificial nature. Clare did love his garden, however, and is merely stating a preference for things that are less contrived. However, all poetry is artifice, made using metre and rhyme, rather than wild words set down anyhow.

But now even nature seems to be leaving Clare: "flitting". He imagines all the grasses, the sky and the breeze are bidding him goodbye. This is partly the effect of the enclosures, but it is also to do with Clare's own emotions and depression at leaving Helpston for Northborough, a move which took him away from childhood scenes and landscapes. He did write some fine poems after the move, but there is no denying that it affected his mental state adversely.

The third stanza contains a personification of beauty, who was his constant companion when he was outdoors. He worshipped her and drank stream water to her health. The line "Love turned e'en water into wine" refers to Christ's miracle at the wedding at Cana. Clare's pantheism is strong here, and even the fields seemed "more than Edens", clouds were "other-country-mountains" and even the "rutty lanes had no compare". Clare is sorrowful that he has lost his sense of wonder at the world of nature.

One of the reasons for this is the stripping of the land during the enclosures. The stream is "naked" because the plants which grew around it have been weeded out, including the brambles. Such acts have banished his goddess, Beauty, and he does not know where to find her now. The imagery is heartbreaking: "The sky hangs o'er a broken dream." This suggests that formerly the land held so much wonder for Clare and now all is gone, taking poetry with it. His "fading vision" no longer sees mushrooms as "fairy bowers" with "marble pillars"; now all he sees are "withered stalks". In the final stanzas, his visions become apocalyptic, night replaces day and friendship is "burned away", has become nothing more than a pretence; he has lost all hope and imagination. This bleak vision links to the poem 'Remembrances', but differs from it in that it mourns a loss of the ability to see things as Clare used to, whereas in 'Remembrances' the things themselves have been destroyed and only memories remain.

'The Eternity of Nature', in the final section of the Everyman selection, offers a contrasting argument. His sense of wonder fully intact, Clare is in awe of the patterns of nature:

> With the odd number five strange nature's laws
> Plays many freaks nor once mistakes the cause,
> And in the cowslip peeps this very day
> Five spots appear which time ne'er wears away,
> Nor once mistakes the counting – look within
> Each peep and five nor more nor less is seen.

He develops his argument with many more examples: birds tend to lay five eggs, bindweed flowers have five lines, bryony[2] has star-shaped flowers with five points. He calls five a "mystic number" and God's design, ordered by "that superior power". The pentangle,[3] an ancient symbol of protection, has five points and stands for earth, air, fire and water, plus spirit. It also stands for the five senses. The motif of the number five is first introduced early on in the poem when Clare is praising the cowslip for its tenacity. He notices its "five crimson spots" on its petals.

The tenacity of flowers is an interesting conundrum because they are frail, delicate and easily cut down on the surface, but the roots are difficult to destroy. The daisy and the cowslip keep returning despite their small size and their continual destruction by mankind. Clare expresses this poetically, saying the daisy "strikes its little root/Into the lap of time", as though time itself is the nurturing mother for daisies. Down the ages, children will still be able to pick this little flower, as they have done for centuries before. The freshness of Clare's imagery never ceases to delight: "Its little golden bosom frilled with snow". The word "bosom" is a soft, gentle, nurturing word. In Shakespeare it is interchangeable with the heart, so is the seat of emotions. With this lexical choice, Clare suggests that the heart of the daisy is trying with all its might to survive.

Clare's argument that nature transcends kings and queens seems particularly apposite in view of the havoc wreaked on the landscape by the enclosures. Clare feels in touch with something timeless when he spends time noticing nature. Although he is aware that birdsong will outlive poetry –

> The little robin in the quiet glen,
> Hidden from fame and all the sons of men,
> Sings unto time a pastoral and gives
> A music that lives on and ever lives

– he nevertheless hopes his poems will still find someone to love them "if I touch aright that quiet tone". Clare is exploring the nature of his own poetry here, realising that he is capturing something timeless to share with future generations, matching the robin's natural song with his own crafted verses. Nature seems to him both mysterious and carefully patterned, beyond our knowledge yet open for us to observe and love.

'Shadows of Taste' is a discursive poem in which Clare explores the idea of preference, both in animals and in people. Heaney classifies it as a verse-essay.[4] Taste and other abstract ideas were popular topics for essays; for example Hazlitt, whom Clare had met in London, wrote an essay 'On Taste' in 1819. Clare wrote this poem in 1820, offering his own take on the topic. Clare is delightfully opinionated and knowledgeable about the things that matter to him. This articulate work gives the lie to those who label Clare 'the peasant poet'. Heaney claims for Clare that

> For all his reputation as a peasant poet, Clare had mastered the repertoire of prescribed styles and skills: nowadays a poet as capable and informed as this would probably be head-hunted to teach a graduate workshop … [5]

While Heaney admires the skill, for him the Clare poems that "still make a catch in the breath and establish a positive bodily hold on the reader"[6] are his rougher, more rustic poems.

That said, 'The Shadows of Taste' has much to recommend it. Typically Clare begins by considering the choices birds make "for joy" when deciding where to build their nests, describing different examples with his wonderful swooping language:

> And the bold eagle which man's fear enshrouds
> Would, could he lodge it, house upon the clouds

Flowers, too, he invests with "wisdom" where they choose to grow, from "leaf-darkened woods" to "barren roads", before moving on to insects in "wild disorder". He likens humans to insects because we too are restless, although our "thoughts scale heaven". Humans have varied taste; some do not even notice the "sweetest scenes". Tastes differ:

> Minds spring as various as the leaves of trees,
> To follow taste and all her sweets explore
> And Edens make where deserts spread before.

But Clare suggests that it is our preferences that hold the keys to our pleasures. One Eden is poetry. It is fascinating to the Clare scholar to read his personal views of poetry. First he discusses the way poetry can elevate common sights, as the face of a pretty girl seen in a crowd can be even lovelier in the poem written after the event. Poetry can not only enhance but preserve such things as birdsong and blossom. Clare introduces the section with the phrase "poesy's spells" and develops the metaphor of magic in the line: "A blossom in its witchery of bloom". Poetry is magical in its transformative ability, and so this imagery is apt.

Poetry appeals to the senses, making the reader see and feel the landscape. Clare comments on the notion of the sublime, which was popular at the time. For him "the true sublime" is not a staged landscape but a poem that is true to nature.

He moves on to consider different fashions in poetry, singling out for praise John Donne's "old homely gold" and Pope's "smooth rhymes", which he compares to the regular chime of a cathedral bell. He is less keen on contemporary poetry which seems to him "half prose, half verse". Science is also considered. This was a fairly new topic in Clare's time, and was the focus of much interest amongst all classes. He contrasts the mindless hunting by children to the explorations of the scientists as they go rambling about, becoming excited by the discovery of lichen, moss or insects. The tendency to murder their finds for their collections is less pleasing to Clare, and is expressed in the strong language he employs:

> And minds of different moods will oft condemn
> His taste as cruel – such the deeds to them –
> While he unconscious gibbets butterflies
> And strangles beetles all to make us wise.

Clare's irony in the phrase "to make us wise" leaves us in no doubt what he thinks about these naturalists' collections. By contrast he himself loves nature for itself. The penultimate section begins:

> Some in recordless rapture love to breathe
> Nature's wild Eden, wood and field and heath;
> In common blades of grass his thoughts will raise
> A world of beauty to admire and praise ...

It is the combination of natural beauty that makes a place truly sublime, and flowers are more than just their scent, butterflies more than pretty wings. In the meadow they show their true beauty, not pinned down on a board, reduced to specimens:

> There hath the flower its dwelling place and there
> The butterfly goes dancing through the air.

A specimen is just a "withered thought" and if these "beings" are taken from their home: "They are but shadows of the things they seem." Almost as bad are those who prefer gardens to nature, who want to tame and weed, allowing art to overtake wild beauty (see the opening section of 'Decay'). Their need to control nature mystifies Clare, who sensibly concludes that good taste is a matter of opinion. Taste is like the rays of the sun, all joining together to make a "proud halo". Our taste enlivens our days and makes us happy. Clare's achievement in this poem is to control the discursive argument while writing lines of great beauty, holding it all together with rhyming couplets in iambic pentameter.

These three poems show Clare could intellectualise in his writing as effectively as any of the other Romantic poets praised for their skills by contemporary critics. They show his versatility, the breadth of his reading, how his thought-processes worked. He too could draw on classical allusion when it suited his purposes. Clare holds his readers in "poesy's spells".

NOTES

1 Quoted in Chambers' essay 'A Love for Every Simple Weed', in *John Clare in Context* (Cambridge University Press, 1994).

2 A climbing plant with white flowers followed by red berries.

3 Sometimes called a pentagram, it is more than just a five-pointed star in that the five points are joined by internal lines.

4 In 'John Clare: A Bi-centenary Lecture', in *John Clare in Context.*

5 Ibid.

6 Ibid.

# 21

# The poet in his joy

In the final section of the Everyman selection, there is a group of poems about memory and how Clare sees himself. The sonnet 'Glinton Spire' focuses on a landmark which is significant to him, symbolising in part his love for Mary Joyce, who lived in Glinton. Another sonnet, 'To John Clare' looks towards home and family, 'The Peasant Poet', 'To be Placed at the Back of his Portrait' and 'Memory' are all poems which attempt to write Clare's epitaph.

'Glinton Spire' could easily stand beside Wordsworth's great sonnet to the city of London, 'Composed upon Westminster Bridge'. Like Wordsworth's sonnet, 'Glinton Spire' invests a significance in landmarks, which inspires people and personifies the scene. Glinton church has a tapered spire which dominates "the level landscape". In a fairly flat landscape, such a spire could be seen from a long way. For Clare, the spire radiates beauty, blessing all around. The sonnet is written very fluently using flexible lines with many enjambments which render the rhyme scheme subtle and enhance the musical movement. Throughout the poem, Clare addresses the spire as an old friend, by choosing the personal mode of address, 'thy'. The spire has been there all of Clare's life and signifies happy memories for him.

'To John Clare' begins like a letter, enquiring after the health of 'honest John'. John Clare's son of the same name was born in 1826, and it is possible that the poem is addressed to him. His father is imagining what he might be doing at home now spring has come. Half of the sonnet is devoted to birds, in particular the robin and the cockerel, which Clare describes in detail, with a humorous line about how the cockerel seems to favour some hens over others:

> And the old cock with wattles and red comb
> Struts with the hens and seems to like some best,
> Then crows and looks about for little crumbs
> Swept out by little folks an hour ago.

The scene is familiar, domestic and comforting; all is well and everything in its place, boys go out to play and the bookseller brings new stories. Many of the things Clare holds dear are included: home, books, birds and domestic animals, daisies. John Lucas comments:

> He may be writing to his son, John, but more likely he's writing to himself. In imagination he's at home, all around him the dailiness of things, a little world of teeming particularity.[1]

This is a comforting thought, because it is one of the last poems Clare wrote before he died in 1864. There is no trace of the angst that presses on him in his darkest moments. Yet at around the same time he wrote to James Hipkins that he had 'nothing to communicate or tell of & why I am shut up I don't know'.[2] He had not lost his ability to write poetry. The sonnet is technically flawless with an alternate rhyme scheme. Jonathan Bate commends its 'pattern of repetition and variation'.[3] The arrival of the pedlar with his books signals a turn from outdoors to indoors as the children leave their games to 'look at the new number just laid down' – the number of books spread out on the table for them to peruse. Memories of home and of Clare's own childhood must have been a comfort to him when he wrote this delightful poem.

'The Peasant Poet' was not given this title by Clare, and the poem does not call him a peasant poet, although he was introduced to the world, as 'The Northamptonshire peasant poet'. He may have been a peasant in his life's station and the rigid class system of the time, but the poem makes a very clear distinction. He was certainly 'a Peasant in his daily cares', but the last line tells us firmly that he was 'The Poet in his joy'. The definite article, 'the' as opposed to the indefinite article 'a', shows that 'The Poet' is how he sees himself, and it is how his readers now view him. The class system is largely swept away and modern eyes are largely unbiased about who can be a poet. Clare's body of work, 4,000 poems, tells us he was 'The Poet' and a very accomplished one indeed.

This poem is Clare writing his own epitaph. This is how he wants to be remembered. He chooses one of his favourite forms, the ballad (although the first line is a foot shorter than usual), to tell us what his poetic agenda is. The poem has a gentle, fluid movement through all the things he loved to write about:

He loved the brook's soft sound,
The swallow swimming by;
He loved the daisy-covered ground,
The cloud-bedappled sky.

He describes the flight of the swallow with a lovely metaphor and the language is full of music, from the repetition of 'loved' the full round vowels in the first line, the consonance of the letter 'w' in the second line, and the antithesis of ground and sky each with their different coverings. The alternate rhyme scheme provides further harmonies.

He develops the idea of pantheism in the middle eight lines, linking God with particular places or events, such as the storm representing the 'voice of God', and his love for the animals that God created. Features of the landscape, such as a particular rock, make him think of Moses from the Bible, leading his people from slavery to the Promised Land. It is interesting to see Clare's assessment of himself in the penultimate couplet:

A silent man in life's affairs,
A thinker from a Boy.

The second line is true. He admits in his autobiographical writings that:

> I grew so fond of being alone at last that my mother was fain to force me into company for the neighbours had assured her mind into the fact that I was no better than crazy.

However, the first of these lines is belied by the fact that he wrote many poems 'on life's affairs' such as the land enclosures. Perhaps it would be more accurate to say he was silenced because many of his best poems were not published for fear of the offence they might give to those of a higher class. Or perhaps Clare simply means he was never a gossiper. This poem is an idealised view of Clare's life but a sound assessment of his writing, and a beautifully crafted lyric as well, as is 'To be Placed at the Back of his Portrait'.

The latter is another poem written by Clare in the third person about himself. The poem is structured with a refrain which starts every stanza except the last, when it occurs half-way through, as it does in the opening stanza also, to produce a coda. He chooses the word 'bard', a word of Celtic origin referring to someone who composes and sings verses. It is often applied to Shakespeare, whose work Clare greatly admired. It is an appropriate lexical choice for Clare, whose own poems are close to music and who was a lover of music all his life. With it he couples less grand subjects, making himself variously "Bard of the mossy cot", "Bard of the fallow field", "Bard of the wild flowers", "Bard o' the sheep pen", and "Bard o' the mossy shed". These are accurate titles for a poet who could always write well about common things. With Clare's poems the mud and rain, the hovels and sheds, weeds and flowers alike get a hearing. The shyness of the title, asking for the poem to be behind his picture for someone to discover, is balanced by the hope that he will be "known through all ages" and, in the last stanza, "Live on for ages". He hopes he has made the daisies immortal in his poems. There is the sense that he was married to Nature, that she is widowed by his death.

Throughout this poem, threaded through it like daisy chains, are many topics unregarded by others: the 'fallow' field is one left unfarmed that year; wild flowers, the rain, the heath, wild birds, cattle and sheep, hovels, a wren (the smallest of birds), daisies. The gentle alternate rhyme scheme includes many vowel sounds, contributing to the soft loving tone. Clare is saying his goodbyes to all the things he made poetry from, and it is the tenderest of farewells.

The final poem in 'Memory' in the Everyman selection is from *A Midsummer Cushion,* written before many of the others in this section, 'John Clare, Poet'. It is a Shakespearian sonnet in style, with a final couplet and an intricate rhyme scheme: *ababbacaacacdd.* Having only four rhyme sounds makes this poem very melodic, particularly with the long vowel sounds most of the rhyme words include. Clare longs for some part of his spirit to survive. He hopes to be remembered by his friends. These are wishes most people share, so that the poem is a comforting one to read. Repetition is built into the structure: "I would not … I would not … I feign would have … " are Clare's three wishes, and the first two include the negative word 'not', which is developed in lines six and seven with the word 'nothing'. The first eight lines define what he does not want to happen when he dies, and the remaining six express what he hopes for: a friend to shed a few tears over his grave. This octet/sestet structure to the argument is Petrarchan-style sonnet form, but Clare also has a turn in the argument, Shakespearian-style, in the final couplet:

> … but such that keep
> Past memories warm with deeds of other years
> And pay to friendship some few friendly tears.

The poem ends on a comforting note; after all the worries of the first eight lines, the wish for a friend to visit his grave answers the worry in lines four and five that he might be buried in some unfamiliar place where no one he knew could come to the grave to pay respect. In the event, his body was brought home to Helpston and buried in the churchyard not far from his parents' graves. Clare would be gratified to know that every year the local children place midsummer cushions around his grave during the annual John Clare festival.

Jonathan Bate's work *The Song of the Earth*[4] consolidated the notion of eco-criticism, which is a way of examining literature by exploring its relationship to the earth and to nature. There is a growing interest in the welfare of the planet and in the way the landscape has been changed, often for the worse, by human endeavour. Clare was writing poems about this topic long before such things were thought of. His work is admired for its range, its accomplished craft, its relationship with the landscape which inspired it, and its originality. He stood up for his own style in the face of constant criticism and editorial tampering. He has been proved right, and his best work is as fresh now as when it was first drafted. He achieved his objective:

> Bard o' the mossy shed,
> Live on for ages;
> Daisies bloom by thy bed
> And live in thy pages.[5]

The daisy was a symbol of hope, innocence and eternity for Clare. Over 150 years after his death, his reputation is secure.

NOTES

1 *John Clare*, Writers and their Work (Northcote House, 1994).

2 Clare's last letter can be seen displayed in Clare Cottage.

4 *John Clare: A Biography* (Picador, 2003).

4 Picador, 2000.

5 From 'To be Placed at the Back of his Portrait'.

# Further reading

## Other selections of Clare's poems

*I Am, The Selected Poetry of John Clare*, edited by Jonathan Bate (Farrar, Straus and Giroux, 2005).

*John Clare The Midsummer Cushion*, edited by Kelsey Thornton and Anne Tibble (Carcanet, 1990).

*Poems of John Clare's Madness*, edited by Geoffrey Grigson (Routledge, 1949).

*John Clare*, selected by Paul Farley (Faber and Faber, 2007).

*The Wood is Sweet*, edited by David Powell (The John Clare Society, 2005).

## Critical works

Jonathan Bate, *The Song of the Earth* (Picador, 2000).

Timothy Brownlow, *John Clare and a Picturesque Landscape* (Clarendon Press, 1983).

George Deacon, *John Clare and the Folk Tradition* (Sinclair Browne, 1983).

John Goodridge (ed.), *The Independent Spirit: John Clare and the Self-Taught Tradition* (The John Clare Society and The Margaret Grainer Memorial Trust, 1994).

Hugh Haughton, Adam Phillips and Geoffrey Summerfield (eds), *John Clare in Context* (Cambridge University Press, 1994).

John Lucas, *John Clare*, Writers and their Work (Northcote House, 1994).

Mark Storey (ed.), *Clare: The Critical Heritage* (Routledge, 1973).

## Biographies

Jonathan Bate, *John Clare: A Biography* (Picador, 2003).

Arnold Clay, *'Itching after Rhyme': A Life of John Clare* (Parapress, 2000).

## Autobiographies and prose

Eric Robinson (ed.), *John Clare's Autobiographical Writings* (Oxford University Press, 1983).

Eric Robinson and David Lawrence (eds), *John Clare by Himself* (Carcanet 2002).

Mark Storey (ed.), *Selected Letters of John Clare* (Clarendon Press, 1988).

## GREENWICH EXCHANGE BOOKS

## STUDENT GUIDE LITERARY SERIES

The Greenwich Exchange Student Guide Literary Series is a collection of essays on major or contemporary serious writers in English and selected European languages. The series is for the student, the teacher and the 'common reader' and is an ideal resource for libraries. The *Times Educational Supplement* praised these books, saying, "The style of [this series] has a pressure of meaning behind it. Readers should learn from that … If art is about selection, perception and taste, then this is it."

The series includes:
**Antonin Artaud** by Lee Jamieson (978-1-871551-98-3)
**W.H. Auden** by Stephen Wade (978-1-871551-36-5)
**Jane Austen** by Pat Levy (978-1-871551-89-1)
**Honoré de Balzac** by Wendy Mercer (978-1-871551-48-8)
**Louis de Bernières** by Rob Spence (978-1-906075-13-2)
**William Blake** by Peter Davies (978-1-871551-27-3)
**The Brontës** by Peter Davies (978-1-871551-24-2)
**Robert Browning** by John Lucas (978-1-871551-59-4)
**Lord Byron** by Andrew Keanie (978-1-871551-83-9)
**Samuel Taylor Coleridge** by Andrew Keanie (978-1-871551-64-8)
**Joseph Conrad** by Martin Seymour-Smith (978-1-871551-18-1)
**William Cowper** by Michael Thorn (978-1-871551-25-9)
**Charles Dickens** by Robert Giddings (987-1-871551-26-6)
**Emily Dickinson** by Marnie Pomeroy (978-1-871551-68-6)
**John Donne** by Sean Haldane (978-1-871551-23-5)
**Elizabethan Love Poets** by John Greening (978-1-906075-52-1)
**Ford Madox Ford** by Anthony Fowles (978-1-871551-63-1)
**Sigmund Freud** by Stephen Wilson (978-1-906075-30-9)
**The Stagecraft of Brian Friel** by David Grant (978-1-871551-74-7)
**Robert Frost** by Warren Hope (978-1-871551-70-9)
**Patrick Hamilton** by John Harding (978-1-871551-99-0)
**Thomas Hardy** by Sean Haldane (978-1-871551-33-4)
**Seamus Heaney** by Warren Hope (978-1-871551-37-2)
**Joseph Heller** by Anthony Fowles (978-1-871551-84-6)
**George Herbert** By Neil Curry and Natasha Curry (978-1-906075-40-8)
**Gerard Manley Hopkins** by Sean Sheehan (978-1-871551-77-8)
**James Joyce** by Michael Murphy (978-1-871551-73-0)

**Philip Larkin** by Warren Hope (978-1-871551-35-8)
**Laughter in the Dark – The Plays of Joe Orton** by Arthur Burke (978-1-871551-56-3)
**George Orwell** by Warren Hope (978-1-871551-42-6)
**Sylvia Plath** by Marnie Pomeroy (978-1-871551-88-4)
**Poets of the First World War** by John Greening (978-1-871551-79-2)
**Alexander Pope** by Neil Curry (978-1-906075-23-1)
**Marcel Proust** by Derwent May (978-1-906075-76-7)
**Restoration Drama** by Sean Elliott (978-1-906075-79-8)
**Philip Roth** by Paul McDonald (978-1-871551-72-3)
**Shakespeare's *A Midsummer Night's Dream*** by Matt Simpson (978-1-871551-90-7)
**Shakespeare's *As You Like It*** by Matt Simpson (978-1-906075-46-0)
**Shakespeare's *Hamlet*** by Peter Davies (978-1-906075-12-5)
**Shakespeare's *Julius Caesar*** by Matt Simpson (978-1-906075-37-8)
**Shakespeare's *King Lear*** by Peter Davies (978-1-871551-95-2)
**Shakespeare's *Macbeth*** by Matt Simpson (978-1-871551-69-3)
**Shakespeare's *The Merchant of Venice*** by Alan Ablewhite (978-1-871551-96-9)
**Shakespeare's *Much Ado about Nothing*** by Matt Simpson (978-1-906075-01-9)
**Shakespeare's Non-Dramatic Poetry** by Martin Seymour-Smith (978-1-871551-22-8)
**Shakespeare's *Othello*** by Matt Simpson (978-1-871551-71-6)
**Shakespeare's *Romeo and Juliet*** by Matt Simpson (978-1-906075-17-0)
**Shakespeare's Second Tetralogy: *Richard II–Henry V*** by John Lucas (978-1-871551-97-6)
**Shakespeare's Sonnets** by Martin Seymour-Smith (978-1-871551-38-9)
**Shakespeare's *The Tempest*** by Matt Simpson (978-1-871551-75-4)
**Shakespeare's *Twelfth Night*** by Matt Simpson (978-1-871551-86-0)
**Shakespeare's *The Winter's Tale*** by John Lucas (978-1-871551-80-8)
**Percy Bysshe Shelley** by Andrew Keanie (978-1-871551-59-0)
**Tobias Smollett** by Robert Giddings (978-1-871551-21-1)
**Alfred, Lord Tennyson** by Michael Thorn (978-1-871551-20-4)
**Dylan Thomas** by Peter Davies (978-1-871551-78-5)
**William Wordsworth** by Andrew Keanie (978-1-871551-57-0)
**W.B. Yeats** by John Greening (978-1-871551-34-1)

## FOCUS ON SERIES

(ISBN prefix 978-1-906075 applies to all the following titles):

**Jane Austen:** ***Mansfield Park*** by Anthony Fowles (61-3)
**James Baldwin:** ***Go Tell It on the Mountain*** by Neil Root (44-6)
**William Blake:** ***Songs of Innocence and Experience*** by Matt Simpson (26-2)
**Charlotte Brontë:** ***Jane Eyre*** by Philip McCarthy (60-6)
**Emily Brontë:** ***Wuthering Heights*** by Matt Simpson (10-1)
**Truman Capote:** ***Breakfast at Tiffany's*** by Neil Root (53-8)
**Angela Carter:** ***The Bloody Chamber and Other Stories*** by Angela Topping (25-5)
***The Poetry of John Clare*** by Angela Topping (48-4)
**George Eliot:** ***Middlemarch*** by John Axon (06-4)
**T.S. Eliot:** ***The Waste Land*** by Matt Simpson (09-5)
**F. Scott Fitzgerald:** ***The Great Gatsby*** by Peter Davies (29-3)
**Michael Frayn:** ***Spies*** by Angela Topping (08-8)
***The Poetry of Robert Graves*** by Michael Cullup (60-9)
**Thomas Hardy:** ***Poems of 1912–13*** by John Greening (04-0)
**Thomas Hardy:** ***Tess of the D'Urbervilles*** by Philip McCarthy (45-3)
***The Poetry of Tony Harrison*** by Sean Sheehan (15-6)
***The Poetry of Ted Hughes*** by John Greening (05-7)
**Aldous Huxley:** ***Brave New World*** by Neil Root (41-5)
**James Joyce:** ***A Portrait of the Artist as a Young Man*** by Matt Simpson (07-1)
**John Keats:** ***Isabella; or, the Pot of Basil, The Eve of St Agnes, Lamia*** **and** ***La Belle Dame sans Merci*** by Andrew Keanie (27-9)
***The Poetry of Mary Leapor*** by Stephen Van-Hagen (35-4)
**V.S. Naipaul:** ***A Bend in the River*** by John Harding (74-3)
**Harold Pinter** by Lee Jamieson (16-3)
**Jean Rhys:** ***Wide Sargasso Sea*** by Anthony Fowles (34-7)
***The Poetry of Jonathan Swift*** by Stephen Van-Hagen (57-6)
**Edward Thomas** by John Greening (28-6)
**Wordsworth and Coleridge:** ***Lyrical Ballads*** **(1798)** by Andrew Keanie (20-0)

Other subjects covered by Greenwich Exchange books:
**Biography**
**Education**
**Philosophy**